Our God Is a Consuming Fire

Michael Greed

WESTBOW·
P R E S S
A DIVISION OF THOMAS NELSON
& ZONDERVAN

Unless otherwise indicated, all Scripture quotations are
taken from the Holy Bible, New International Version®
Anglicized, NIV® Copyright © 1979, 1984, 2011 by Biblica,
Inc.® Used by permission. All rights reserved worldwide.

Cover illustration: *Fructify*, by Susana Morvan. Used with permission.
Author photo by Emma-Liisa Greed. Used with permission.

WestBow Press books may be ordered through
booksellers or by contacting:

WestBow Press
A Division of Thomas Nelson & Zondervan
1663 Liberty Drive
Bloomington, IN 47403
www.westbowpress.com
1 (866) 928-1240

ISBN: 978-1-4908-5532-5 (sc)
ISBN: 978-1-4908-5531-8 (e)

Library of Congress Control Number: 2014918069

Printed in the United States of America.

WestBow Press rev. date: 10/28/2014

Contents

"The LORD your God is a consuming
fire, a jealous God." (Deut. 4.24)

"Let us be thankful, and so worship God
acceptably with reverence and awe, for our
'God is a consuming fire'." (Heb. 12.28-29)

"Then they will go away to eternal
punishment, but the righteous to
eternal life." Jesus (Matt. 25.46)

Preface

It has taken me more than 30 years to write this book. In the 1980s I decided I ought to write a book about hell. I had been reflecting on this topic a lot since the traditional picture of hell, as handed down by my evangelical tradition, seemed to be in line neither with the straightforward meaning of Scripture nor my understanding of the character of God. I wrote substantial notes at that time, filed them away, and that was it. In the 1990s I went over my notes, keyboarded them into the computer and added a load more. But that's all it became: an increased number of notes. More comments on my own pilgrimage can be found in chapter 8, which contains some of the earliest material in this book.

In 1996 David Pawson published *The Road to Hell: Everlasting Torment or Annihilation?* (Pawson, 1996a). Some eight years later *"Hell Under Fire: Modern Scholarship Reinvents Eternal Punishment"* (Morgan & Peterson, 2004) was published, with contributions from a number of evangelical scholars. While all the authors argued in favour of everlasting torment, I took particular issue with the chapter written by J. I. Packer. So, in the 1990s my file of notes expanded with comments on and critique of David Pawson's position, and then in the 2000s as I interacted with J. I. Packer's views.

It was the publication of *Love wins* by Rob Bell (2011) that gave me the incentive to take my notes and translate them into a coherent manuscript. Although Bell and I do not hold identical positions, I do not interact with his writings in this book. Rather, I find it preferable to interact with those who hold positions that are quite contrary to mine.

Now, as I write these lines it is May 2014. Since WestBow Press have expressed interest in publishing this book I have examined, edited, expanded and, I hope, improved the manuscript. One new chapter has been added, chapter 14. It has been an interesting exercise. I find that my views have remained substantially the same on this topic since the 1980s, although my understanding has developed and matured, as I have studied the topic further and interacted with literature and discussed ideas with friends. The only detail where I have changed my mind, as it were, is the nature of time in the age to come.

Further books and articles have been written since Morgan & Peterson compiled *Hell Under Fire* in 2004, but I have not come across any new arguments. So although this book is being published ten years after *Hell Under Fire* I am confident that I am bringing fresh insight to issues that are always relevant and worthy of investigation.

What follows, then, was started in the 1980s, developed in the 1990s as I interacted with Pawson and in the 2000s as I interacted with Packer, written up as a coherent manuscript in 2011, then finally expanded and finalised in 2014.

My thanks go to all those who have interacted with me on these issues, from the 1980s to the present, in particular to Ben Chenoweth, Michal Domagala, Teija Greed and Peter Kirk for their valuable feedback on my manuscript, and to Susana Morvan for a cover illustration that matches the content of the book perfectly.

Michael Greed, July 2014

Introduction

I am genuinely confused when well-meaning Christians defend the existence of a hell of eternal torment as if their life and faith depend upon it. Shouldn't it be a matter of rejoicing if, through faithful and thorough study of the Scriptures, we realise that some of our fore-fathers in the faith were mistaken in this regard; that we do not need to juggle a God of love with a God who throws the majority of humankind into everlasting torment; that we can worship the God of compassion and mercy without having a nagging doubt in the back of our mind: what about compassion and mercy on all those languishing in the torments of hell? The biblical evidence for a hell of eternal torment is at best ambiguous. I would go further and suggest that the biblical evidence makes such a position untenable.

I hold to a high view of Scripture. Like Paul I believe, "All Scripture is God-breathed and is useful for teaching, rebuking, correcting and training in righteousness, so that the servant of God may be thoroughly equipped for every good work." (2 Tim. 3.16-17) Jesus states, "Anyone who sets aside one of the least of these commands and teaches others accordingly will be called least in the kingdom of heaven, but whoever practises and teaches these commands will be called great in the kingdom of heaven." (Matt. 5.19) Therefore I do not approach this topic lightly. Scripture is my starting point, map and compass, and I endeavour to do justice to the text and context of Scripture throughout.

"Hell", as we shall see, does not exist in the Bible. Eternal punishment, yes. A consuming fire, yes. But "hell" in the popularly understand form of everlasting torment has more in common with medieval scaremongering than biblical exegesis. What I find in the Scriptures is something far more awe-inspiring: that which some commentators call "hell" is none other than an activity and manifestation of the LORD God himself, for *our God is a consuming fire.*

Read on…

1

The Tree of Life

In the beginning God created the heavens and the earth. Genesis 2 tells us how the LORD God formed a human being and breathed the breath of life into him. Then we are told that there were two trees in the middle of the garden:

> Now the LORD God had planted a garden in the east, in Eden; and there he put the man he had formed... In the middle of the garden were the tree of life and the tree of the knowledge of good and evil. (Gen. 2.8-9)

The first thing that God says in Genesis 2 relates to these trees. He says:

> You are free to eat from any tree in the garden; but you must not eat from the tree of the knowledge of good and evil, for when you eat from it you will certainly die. (Gen. 2.16-17)

Genesis 3 gives the account of how the man and woman did eat from the tree of the knowledge of good and evil. They did not drop down dead. The text simply states that their eyes were opened and they realised they were naked. Big deal? God had said they would die.

Of course Adam and Eve ate the fruit of the forbidden tree. In addition, their descendants have gone forth and filled the earth (no problems obeying that command), and we still eat the fruit of the forbidden tree. We deceive ourselves if we think God hoped Adam and Eve and all their descendants would for all time resist temptation and refrain from eating the fruit of this tree. God was – and still is – in control. Genesis 3.9 onwards is not God's hastily thrown together contingency plan because things had gone wrong.

After Adam and Eve (and we) have eaten God says,

> "The man has now become like one of us, knowing good and evil. He

must not be allowed to reach out his
hand and take also from the tree of
life and eat, and live forever." So the
LORD God banished him from the
Garden of Eden. (Gen. 3.22-23)

Because mankind has eaten from the fruit of the
first tree (the tree of the knowledge of good and
evil) God ensures that we cannot eat from the fruit
of the second tree (the tree of life). The precise
nature of the tree of the knowledge of good and evil
is not our concern here. God's reaction is sufficient:
mankind has become "like one of us, knowing
good and evil". We are like gods. Or rather, it
is almost as if we have become members of the
godhead – "like one of us". In making sure that we
cannot eat from the tree of life, God ensures that
mankind cannot live forever. God explicitly states
that the man must not be allowed to live forever.
That means we are mortal. We die. We are not
immortal. We do not live for ever.

The serpent was right. Adam and Eve did not die
when they ate the fruit of the forbidden tree. But
the serpent was also wrong. Because they ate the
fruit of that tree they were denied the fruit of the
other tree. Without eating of the tree of life we
cannot live for ever. The banishment from the
garden of Eden is not phrased as a punishment.
They were banished to stop them eating of the tree

of life. Cherubim and a flaming sword were placed at the entrance to the garden so as to ensure that no one had access to the tree of life (Gen. 3.24).

That is where the Genesis story ends. Only those who have eaten of the tree of life will live for ever. But access to the tree of life is barred. No one has eaten of the tree of life; no one will live for ever. Apart from some metaphorical references in *Proverbs*, we see no more of the tree of life in the entire Old Testament. It is forbidden and forgotten. As we continue through the Scriptures and study the New Testament we could be forgiven for thinking that the tree of life has been entirely lost. But then, suddenly, right at the end of the story, in the last chapter of the last book, *Revelation*, we're shown the tree of life again – and it is bearing fruit.

1.1 From Genesis to Revelation

Earlier in the book of Revelation (2.7) Jesus (through John) says, "To the one who is victorious, I will give the right to eat from the tree of life, which is in the paradise of God."

Is access possible after all? Who are these victorious ones? The possibilities are tantalizing. Then in Revelation 22 we are given more detail. The angel shows John the river of the water of life which flows down from the throne of God and of the Lamb. The narrative continues:

> On each side of the river stood the tree of life, bearing twelve crops of fruit, yielding its fruit every month. And the leaves of the tree are for the healing of the nations. (Rev. 22.2)

The fruit is abundant. Fresh fruit every month. But we are still not told who has the right to eat it. We note too that such are the life-giving properties of this tree that its leaves bring healing to the nations. The nations too are right there in the holy city enjoying the healing which the tree of life gives them.

It isn't until the very last page of the Bible that we are told who may eat the fruit of the tree of life:

> Blessed are those who wash their robes, that they may have the right to the tree of life and may go through the gates into the city. (Rev. 22.14)

The "victorious" ones of Revelation 2.7 are here identified as "those who wash their robes". Those who wash their robes have access to the tree of life and may enter the city, the new Jerusalem which has come down from heaven. In the context of Revelation 2, the "victorious" ones are those who have persevered in following Jesus faithfully. The washed robes of Revelation 22 are picking up a theme from chapter 7 where John sees "a great multitude that no one could count, from every nation, tribe, people and language" (v. 9). One of the elders tells John that these are they who "have washed their robes and made them white in the blood of the Lamb" (v. 14). This uncountable crowd from every language and culture are all there eating the fruit of the tree of life, on the banks of the river of life.

There we have it: the beginning and the end of the story. In the beginning mankind is banished from access to the tree of life. At the end the countless multitude of those who are victorious and have washed their robes may eat of the tree of life and live for ever. Hang on, you may ask, we've looked at the first three chapters of the Bible and the last chapter. What happens in between?

2

Hell and Gehenna

What happens in between is the result of mankind eating the fruit of the tree of the knowledge of good and evil. Because we ate of this tree we are forbidden from eating of the other tree. There are two results, then, of Adam and Eve's disobedience: Firstly their eyes were opened (Gen. 3.7) and secondly immortality was denied to them. This is shown by the fact that they were banished from access to the tree of life (Gen 3.22-23). The result of their action was death, not directly because their eyes were opened but because they were denied access to the tree of life. The result is still death. They, and we, do not live for ever. They, and we, have not eaten of the tree of life. They ate, they died. We eat, we die. Not instantaneously of course, but the result is that we are mortal. As Jesus puts it:

> Do not be afraid of those who kill
> the body but cannot kill the soul.
> Rather, be afraid of the One who can
> destroy both soul and body in hell.
> (Matt. 10.28)

Body and soul – that is the outer and inner person – God can and does destroy a person in "hell". Hell? Bible translators have a lot to answer for.

2.1 Sheol

The Hebrew word *Sheol* is translated as "hell" in some English versions. *Sheol* first appears in the biblical narrative in Genesis 37 where Jacob, thinking his favourite son, Joseph, is dead, wails, "I shall go down to Sheol to my son, mourning."(Gen. 37.35, NRSV) He then repeats the theme when he thinks his second-favourite son, Benjamin, might die: "If you take this one also from me, and harm comes to him, you will bring down my grey hairs in sorrow to Sheol." (Gen. 44.29, NRSV)

Most translations do not translate the word. They simply retain the Hebrew word in the English text (like the NRSV above), or they call it "the realm of the dead" or "the grave" (for example the NIV translation of the same verses). Another example is Psalm 16.10. It reads as follows:

For thou wilt not leave my soul in
hell. (KJV)

For you do not give me up to Sheol.
(NRSV)

Because you will not abandon me to
the realm of the dead. (NIV)

You canceled my ticket to hell. (The
Message)

Sheol is also translated as "the pit" or "the grave"
in other passages. The ancient Israelites did not
have a theology of the afterlife. *Sheol* was simply
the world of the dead, the place dead people go
to, some kind of shadowy, undefined place. It was
neither good nor bad, morally neutral. Where an
English translation of the Old Testament uses the
word "hell" it is most likely to be a rendering of
the Hebrew *Sheol*. Here is another example, from
Proverbs 7.27:

Her house is the way to hell. (KJV)

Her house is the way to Sheol.
(NRSV)

Her house is a highway to the grave.
(NIV)

> She runs a halfway house to hell.
> (The Message)

Hebrew poetry likes to employ parallelism, that is, state the same thing twice using different words. In a verse like Proverbs 7.27 this helps us understand the meaning of the word *Sheol*, where *Sheol* is paralleled with "death":

> Her house is the way to hell, going down to the chambers of death. (KJV)

> Her house is the way to Sheol, going down to the chambers of death. (NRSV)

> Her house is a highway to the grave, leading down to the chambers of death. (NIV)

> She runs a halfway house to hell, fits you out with a shroud and a coffin. (The Message)

All of which is a rather ornate way of saying that she will kill you.

2.2 Hades and Tartaros

When we come to the New Testament there are two Greek words that the KJV, NRSV and NIV translators translate as "hell":

> Gehenna (12 times: Matt. 5.22, 29, 30; 10.28; 18.9; 23.15, 33; Mark 9.43, 45, 47; Luke 12.5; Jas. 3.6)
>
> Tartaros (once: 2 Pet. 2.4)

A third, similar word in the New Testament is *Hades. Hades* is more or less the equivalent of *Sheol* and is found ten times in the New Testament: four times on the lips of Jesus in the Gospels, twice in Acts and four times in Revelation. In the four occurrences in the book of Revelation it is conjoined with Death: for example, Revelation 1.18, "I hold the keys of death and Hades." In the two occurrences in Acts (2.27 and 31) Peter is citing Psalm 16 where the psalmist wrote "Sheol", as already quoted above.

The four occurrences in the Gospels are as follows:

> And you, Capernaum, will you be lifted to the heavens? No, you will go down to Hades. (Matt. 11.23, paralleled in Luke 10.15)

> I tell you that you are Peter, and on
> this rock I will build my church, and
> the gates of Hades will not overcome
> it. (Matt. 16.18)

> In Hades, where he was in torment,
> he looked up and saw Abraham
> far away, with Lazarus by his side.
> (Luke 16.23)

We see here some development of meaning from the Hebrew *Sheol* which is morally neutral. *Hades* is contrasted with heaven, is seen as something which might be antagonistic towards the church, and is a place of torment. Let us note, too, that Jesus holds the keys of *Hades*. *Hades* is not the same as *Gehenna*, it is more or less synonymous with death.

The other term, *Tartaros,* comes from Greek mythology where it was a deep abyss used as a dungeon where the wicked (and in particular the Titans) were imprisoned and tormented. The author of 2 Peter was clearly aware of this mythology, as he writes: "God did not spare angels when they sinned, but sent them to *Tartaros* putting them in chains of darkness to be held for judgment." (2 Pet. 2.4)

2.3 Gehenna

Gehenna was the rubbish tip outside Jerusalem. Most of the New Testament references to it are on the lips of Jesus:

> Anyone who say, "You fool!" will be in danger of the fire of hell. (Matt. 5.22)

> It is better for you to lose one part of your body than for your whole body to be thrown into hell. (Matt. 5.29. Parallels or close parallels in Matt. 5.30; Matt. 18.9; Mark 9.43, 45 and 47)

> Be afraid of the One who can destroy both soul and body in hell. (Matt. 10.28, and close parallel in Luke 12.5)

> Woe to you, teachers of the law and Pharisees, you hypocrites! You travel over land and sea to win a single convert, and when you have succeeded, you make them twice as much a child of hell as you are. (Matt. 23.15)

> You snakes! You brood of vipers! How will you escape being condemned to hell? (Matt. 23.33)

In the letter of James it is a description of the tongue:

> The tongue also is a fire, a world of evil among the parts of the body. It corrupts the whole body, sets the whole course of one's life on fire, and is itself set on fire by hell. (Jas. 3.6)

I have had something of a love-hate relationship with David Pawson's writings. In 1990 he published a book with the title, *Leadership is male*. I disagreed with him. He then published *Once save, always saved?* I entered the book truly agnostic on this topic, and Pawson convinced me. I agreed with him and still do. So when I opened his book *The Road to Hell: everlasting torment or annihilation?* I entered it with an open mind.

As it turned out, Pawson convinced me. I found his arguments for a "traditional hell" so weak and lacking in biblical foundation, that his book confirmed to me that my exegesis of Scripture seemed to be along the right lines. I will discuss some of Pawson's points in the course of this book, but for the moment I will bow to Pawson's greater knowledge of Gehenna. Unlike me, he has been to Israel several times. He has seen Gehenna. Early on in *The Road to Hell* he gives a good description of it:

So how did Jesus 'picture' hell? The answer lies in the name he usually gave to it: Gehenna, which means 'the valley of Hinnom'.

This is a real geographic location, a deep gorge to the west and south of Jerusalem. From it the city is visible, but most of it is invisible to the city. Few tourists visit or are even aware of it.

The valley has a sinister history. At one stage in Israel's idolatrous infidelities it became a centre for the worship of Moloch ... Jeremiah predicted that 'the days are coming, declares the Lord, when people will no longer call this place Topheth or the Valley of Ben Hinnom, but the Valley of Slaughter' (Jer. 9:6).

Partly for this reason and partly because of its convenient location and depth, the valley became the city's garbage dump. The south gate facing the valley is to this day called the 'Dung Gate', which speaks for itself. All the sewage and rubbish of

> a large city was 'thrown into' (note that term) Gehenna.
>
> The waste was kept down in two ways - incineration by fire of what was combustible and ingestion by worms of what was digestible. Steep cliffs confined the heat and the smell (its lowest point was too deep for the sun to penetrate). (Pawson, 1996a, pp. 28-29)

Worms and fire. Sewage and rubbish is thrown into this deep abyss where it is consumed. In Jesus' day, as in Pawson's, "the worms that eat them do not die, and the fire is not quenched" (Mark 9.48). This is Gehenna, this is hell.

In these words from Mark 9 Jesus is quoting Isaiah 66.22-24 where the Lord, through the voice of the prophet, is announcing the permanence of the new heavens and new earth.

> "As the new heavens and the new earth that I make will endure before me," declares the LORD, "so will your name and descendants endure. From one New Moon to another and from one Sabbath to another, all mankind will come and bow down

> before me," says the LORD. "And
> they will go out and look on the
> dead bodies of those who rebelled
> against me; the worms that eat them
> will not die, the fire that burns them
> will not be quenched, and they will
> be loathsome to all mankind." (Isa.
> 66.22-24)

In Isaiah 64 the prophet contrasts "the new heavens and the new earth" and "your name and your descendants" on the one hand, which will endure, with "the dead bodies of those who rebelled against me" on the other hand which will not endure.

The new heavens, the new earth, your name and your descendants endure, whereas those who rebel against God do not endure. Those who endure look on the dead bodies of those who do not endure.

The worm does not die and the fire will not be quenched: these are the agents of God's punishment – as Pawson eloquently puts it, "Incineration by fire of what was combustible and ingestion by worms of what was digestible." But – and this is the important point – those who are consumed and ingested die. They cease to exist. The rebel has not endured.

2.4 Hell in God

"In the beginning God created heaven, earth and hell."

No, that's not what the text says.

> In the beginning God created the
> heavens and the earth. (Gen. 1.1)

The Scriptures never say that God created hell. What, then, is hell? Where did it come from? It would be quite out of place for the creation narratives in Genesis 1 and 2 to state that God created hell, because there wasn't any sin in the world yet. We see the first fruits of sin in Genesis 4, where Cain kills his brother Abel (v. 6-8) and in the statement of Cain's descendent, Lamech (v. 23-24). Genesis 6 then begins with a summary statement about the "wickedness of the human race" and the evil that is in the human heart (Gen. 6.5). Did God create hell at this point? No, he sent a flood, saying, "I will wipe from the face of the earth the human race I have created" (Gen. 6.7). Whilst Noah, his family and two of each animal species survived, every other living thing "perished" (Gen. 7.21). Those who died in the flood did not go to hell, they simply perished.

Although we do not find hell in the Old Testament, we do find fire there. The LORD God is described as a "consuming fire" (Deut. 4.24). This is quoted in Hebrews 12:

> Therefore, since we are receiving a kingdom that cannot be shaken, let us be thankful, and so worship God acceptably with reverence and awe, for our "God is a consuming fire." (v. 28-29)

In chapter 4 we will look more thoroughly at how the LORD God is equated with fire in the Bible. God, the consuming fire, consumes all that is not holy: the unholy parts of his people whom he has made holy (a "refiner's fire" – Mal. 3.2), and the entirety of those who are not holy. There is a popular misconception in some quarters that the fate of those outside of God is eternal torment or torture. Those who hold this opinion believe there is another fire that is also eternal, that is somehow opposite to God, and that this fire never actually consumes but rather suspends those thrown into it in a state of everlasting torment. I suggest that this is not what the Scriptures teach. The fire that some call "hell" is the same as the "consuming fire" of Deuteronomy 4.24 and Hebrews 12.29 – that is, it is a picture of God's judgement of the wicked. The Scriptures teach that while the location of the lost is eternal, the lost themselves simply die there.

That is, they cease to exist. This is why Gehenna is such a suitable description of it.

Hell was not created by God for the simple reason that hell (so-called) is, in a way, an activity of God himself. "Hell" is the attribute of God that judges sin and wickedness. "Hell", I suggest, is not a place but an expression of an activity of God. Sin and wickedness cannot endure, for only faith, hope and love endure (compare 1 Cor. 13.13). There is no room for sin and wickedness in God's age to come, therefore God burns them up. This is the judgment of God, plainly taught in the Scriptures.

Judgment, however, is not the primary focus of God's overall plan. God's plan is heaven on earth, a prerequisite of which is the destruction of sin and wickedness.

3

Heaven

What is heaven? Heaven is where God lives. There are many references in the Psalms alone that would illustrate this. Here are three examples:

> The LORD looks down from heaven on all mankind to see if there are any who understand, any who seek God. (Ps. 14.2)

> Return to us, God Almighty! Look down from heaven and see! (Ps. 80.14)

> The LORD looked down from his sanctuary on high, from heaven he viewed the earth. (Ps. 102.19)

The Hebrew word normally translated "heaven" is *shamayim* and it is used 416 times in the Old Testament. The Greek word for heaven, *ouranos*, is used 274 times. "Heaven" in Scripture is compared and contrasted with "earth". Heaven is where God dwells, earth is where humankind dwells. This is evident in the psalms cited above: God looks down from heaven and views mankind on the earth.

Jesus begins his ministry by announcing that the Kingdom of Heaven is near. He is on earth (the dwelling place of humankind) and he states that the Kingdom of heaven (the dwelling place of God, where God reigns) is near. Jesus is thus saying that in him the dwelling place of God and the dwelling place of human beings is coming together – a picture picked up in the last chapters of Revelation where heaven and earth come together as one and God's dwelling (heaven) is among humankind (on earth).

This is the intent of the prayer Jesus taught his followers to pray: "Your will be done on earth as it is in heaven." (Matt. 6.10) God's will is done in heaven. God's will is not yet done on earth. Yet Jesus tells his followers to pray that God's will will be done on earth. Where God's will is done the Kingdom of Heaven reigns.

3.1 Heaven is a place on earth

The Kingdom of Heaven, Tom Wright explains, "does not refer to a place, called 'heaven', where God's people will go after death. It refers to the rule of heaven, that is, of God, being brought to bear in the present world." (Wright, 2000, p. 20) A programme of social justice, healing the sick, giving sight to the blind and freedom to the oppressed, giving dignity to men and women, the opportunity to live this life as God its Creator intended – this is bringing in the Kingdom of Heaven, that is, the rule of God. (Compare Luke 4.16-21.) The 1980s pop song was not far wrong:

> Heaven is a place on earth
> They say in heaven love comes first
> We'll make heaven a place on earth
> Ooh heaven is a place on earth.
> (Nowels & Shipley, 1987)

In contrast to the 690 references to "heaven" in the Scriptures, the Greek *Gehenna*, translated "hell" in the NIV occurs 12 times. The Hebrew *Sheol* occurs 66 times, but as we have already observed, *Sheol* is not the same as "hell" and the NIV reflects this by translating it simply as "the grave" or "the realm of the dead", while the REB has "Sheol" and the RSV "the Pit".

"Heaven" and "hell" are not equals in the Scriptures. "Heaven" is paired with "earth". Neither are "eternal life" and "eternal judgment/fire/punishment/destruction" equal. The Greek New Testament uses the phrase "eternal life" (*zoe aionios*) 43 times, and the phrase "eternal judgment/fire/punishment/destruction" six times. That is not to say that the concept of eternal judgment/fire/punishment/destruction is unimportant: three of these six occurrences are on the lips of Jesus himself. But we are wrong if we think the Scriptures give them an equal force or focus. "Eternal life" is a reference to God's age to come. Participation in the coming age is what God has in store for those who trust him.

The phrase "eternal death" – which is a contradiction in terms – never occurs in the Scriptures.

3.2 Eternal

Broadly speaking there are two types of academic research: quantitative and qualitative. Quantitative research focuses on things that can be measured: When? Where? How long? How many? Qualitative research, on the other hand, is more difficult to pin down, focussing as it does on the quality of the item or topic under consideration: Why? How? What kind of? How do I sense or experience...?

The Greek word "eternal" (*aionios*) is often considered only quantitatively, in particular, "How long?" Answer: "For ever." It is therefore popularly though of as being synonymous with "never ending" and "everlasting". Yes, it does embrace this area of meaning, but it is a far wider, richer word, with deep qualitative meaning as well.

The root of the Greek word *aionios* is *aion* which means "age" or "era". If we consider the question, "What kind of?" with reference to eternal/*aionios* the answer might be, "Having the characteristics of something that lasts for an immeasurably long length of time; that is, the opposite of temporary."

We noted above that most occurrences of the word eternal/*aionios* are in the phrase "eternal life/*zoe aionios*". *Aionios* (in one form or another) can be found 71 times in the Greek New Testament, of these 43 are in the phrase "eternal life/*zoe aionios*". Some of the other things described as "eternal" are "things which are not seen" (2 Cor. 4.18), God's dominion (1 Tim. 6.16) and God's glory (1 Pet. 5.10).

We also observed that fire, punishment, judgment and destruction are called eternal (Matt. 18.8; Matt 25.41; Matt 25.46; 2 Thes. 1.9; Heb. 6.2; Jude 1.7). As we show elsewhere in this book (for example, chapter 4), "eternal fire" refers to a manifestation of God himself. The only occurrence of the phrase, "eternal punishment" is at the end of the story of the sheep and the goats (see chapter 13), where we will see that the eternal nature of the punishment is the exclusion from the life of the coming age. Paul's use of the phrase, "eternal destruction" in 2 Thessalonians 1.9 is similar, as he describes it as "shut out from the presence of the Lord and from the glory of his might". "Eternal judgment" in Hebrews 6.2 is part of a list of "elementary teachings". The Bible teaches eternal judgment: the condemnation of the wicked and the eternal life of the righteous.

Moving onto the phrase "eternal life/*zoe aionios*", it refers to the life of the coming age. The life of the present age is temporary, the life of the coming age is eternal. To understand the quality of this eternal life we need to turn to those passages of Scripture which describe our future hope, passages such as,

> They will neither harm nor destroy on all my holy mountain, for the earth will be filled with the knowledge of the LORD as the waters cover the sea. (Isa. 11.9)

> See, I will create new heavens and a new earth. (Isa. 65.17)

The righteous will shine like the sun in the kingdom of their Father. (Matt. 13.43)

I consider that our present sufferings are not worth comparing with the glory that will be revealed in us. For the creation waits in eager expectation for the children of God to be revealed… in hope that the creation itself will be liberated from its bondage to decay and brought into the freedom and glory of the children of God. (Rom. 8.18-21)

We know that if the earthly tent we live in is destroyed, we have a building from God, an eternal house in heaven, not built by human hands. (2 Cor. 5.1)

I heard a loud voice from the throne saying, 'Look! God's dwelling-place is now among the people, and he will dwell with them. They will be his people, and God himself will be with them and be their God. "He will wipe every tear from their eyes. There will be no more death" or mourning or crying or pain, for the

old order of things has passed away.'
(Rev. 21.3-4)

These verses represent entire passages of Scripture, and they are just a sample of what we are told about the life of the age to come. We consider eternal life further in chapter 14, where a whole chapter is devoted to the topic.

4

God revealed as fire

We stated in chapter 2 that "hell" is an attribute of God, an expression of an activity of God. Jesus describes hell in terms of worms that do not die and fire that is not quenched. Are we saying, then, that God is a worm? Is God a literal fire? Of course not. These are metaphors. Fire is a closer or more fitting metaphor than worm and so we find the metaphor "God = Fire" frequently throughout the Scriptures. The point of comparison in Mark 9 is that both consume. The worm and the fire consume. God also consumes.

4.1 Fire in the Mosaic law

"Fire" is a powerful symbol and metaphor for God and it is found throughout the Scriptures.

In Leviticus 6.12-13 it says,

> The fire on the altar must be kept burning; it must not go out. Every morning the priest is to add firewood and arrange the burnt offering on the fire and burn the fat of the fellowship offerings on it. The fire must be kept burning on the altar continuously; it must not go out.

Why was it so important that the fire not go out? OK, the ancient Israelite priests didn't have matches – but fire was all around them. It was no big deal to take some fire from somewhere else in order to start a new fire; or to re-ignite a fire that had gone out. So what's going on here? Why was it so crucial that the fire be kept burning on the altar continuously?

The Mosaic law is packed with symbolism. In it everything means something. The New Testament writers picked up on this – for example the writer to the Hebrews who writes, "The law is only a shadow of the good things that are coming—not the realities themselves" (Heb. 10.1). The sacrificial offering symbolises something; the prayers are a picture of something; the blood represents something else, and so forth.

4.2 Blood, incense, sacrifice

Let's begin with the blood. The life is in the blood. This is stated in Leviticus 17.11. Therefore the eating (or drinking) of blood is forbidden. This became an issue in the New Testament. Were the new Gentile believers required to follow this prohibition? Acts 15.19-29 states *Yes*. Ongoing church practice showed it to be relative. If you live in a community which adheres to this symbolism you follow the rule. But if you don't live in such a community and don't share the same symbolism the rule does not apply. But in the Mosaic law it is clear: the blood = the life.

Another example of symbolic metaphor is the incense. Incense drifts upwards from the sacrifice, and so it's easy to see how it came to mean prayer – see, for example, Psalm 141.1-2. This same image is picked up in Revelation where the gold bowls of incense are the prayers of God's people (Rev. 5.8).

How about the sacrificial offering – what did that represent? The people. It was always clear that the sacrificed animal died instead of the one sacrificing it. See, for example, Leviticus 6.1-7, where the ram dies because of the sin and guilt of the human. An individual sins – in the example in Leviticus 6 they cheat their neighbour. Sin leads to death – but it is not the sinful individual who dies but an animal instead. The individual can go free, forgiven, because a ram has died in his place. The ram has taken his place. This symbolism is picked up powerfully by Paul in Romans 12.1.

Any old animal won't do. The animal needs to be specially chosen, without defect and the right species. More generally than that, the whole animal kingdom is divided up into clean and unclean animals. A whole chapter (Lev. 11) is devoted to defining the distinction. Clean animals are those that have a divided hoof and chew the cud. Those are the ones that can be eaten. Camels, hyraxes and rabbits cannot be eaten because they chew the cud but do not have a divided hoof. The list goes on, with reference to creatures of the seas and streams, birds, insects and a variety of creepy-crawlies. What is the rationale? What is the big deal about divided hooves and chewing the cud? I'm convinced it's entirely arbitrary. Why did God choose Abraham and his descendants, the Jews?

Because they have a divided hoof and chew the cud.

Abraham and the Israelites have a divided hoof and chew the cud. Therefore they are acceptable. That is, God did not choose the Jews because they were more holy or more prestigious or more powerful; nor even because they were less holy, less prestigious and weak. God had a plan and he needed a people, and he picked Abram: "The LORD had said to Abram, 'Go from your country, your people and your father's household to the land I will show you.'" (Gen. 12.1). The only characteristics Abram needed were trust and obedience. That is still the case. You may or may not chew the cud, your hoof may or may not be divided. What matters to God is trust and obedience.

This is the poignancy of Peter's vision in Acts 10. In his vision Peter sees animals, unclean animals, and God instructs him to kill and eat. Peter realises that the message God is communicating to him isn't simply that all animals are acceptable, but that Gentiles too are acceptable – and acceptable as Gentiles. The distinction is no more, the wall that separated Jew from Gentile had been torn down. Paul, addressing Gentiles, puts it this way, "You are no longer foreigners and strangers, but fellow citizens with God's people and also members of his household." (Eph. 2.19)

The sacrifice = the people. The blood = the life. The incense = prayer.

And the fire? The fire = God himself.

4.3 God revealed as fire

Fire in the Mosaic law represents God. There are hints in this direction prior to the exodus narrative – for example, the "smoking brazier with a blazing torch" in Genesis 15.17 with which God makes his first covenant with Abram. Once the exodus narrative begins the link is quite explicit. First of all the God revealed as fire appears to Moses in a burning bush:

> Now Moses was tending the flock of Jethro his father-in-law, the priest of Midian, and he led the flock to the far side of the wilderness and came to Horeb, the mountain of God. [2] There the angel of the Lord appeared to him in flames of fire from within a bush. Moses saw that though the bush was on fire it did not burn up. [3] So Moses thought, 'I will go over and see this strange sight – why the bush does not burn up.'
>
> [4] When the Lord saw that he had gone over to look, God called to him from within the bush, "Moses! Moses!" (Exod. 3.1-4)

Then, once the Israelites have left Egypt, the LORD accompanies his chosen people in a pillar of fire.

> By day the LORD went ahead of them in a pillar of cloud to guide them on their way and by night in a pillar of fire to give them light, so that they could travel by day or night. (Exod. 13.21)

Then the LORD descends on Mount Sinai in fire:

> Mount Sinai was covered with smoke, because the LORD descended on it in fire. The smoke billowed up from it like smoke from a furnace, and the whole mountain trembled violently. (Exod. 19.18)

such that the glory of the Lord "looked like a consuming fire on top of the mountain" (Exod. 24.17).

When God appears to Ezekiel he is a fire (albeit a rather unusual one) – see Ezekiel 1.4-5. When the LORD displayed his might and splendour on Mount Carmel it was in fire – see 1 Kings 18.36-39. After a rainstorm and fleeing south to Horeb (Sinai), Elijah was hoping to meet with God and quite naturally he expected God to appear in fire – see 1 Kings 19.11-12. The fact that God was not in the fire, but in a "gentle whisper" was a major surprise to Elijah. It was not what he expected.

The prophets make frequent reference to God as a fire, or being like a fire, or having the characteristics of fire. See, for example, David's song of thanksgiving in Psalm 18 where smoke rises from the LORD's nostrils, and consuming fire comes from his mouth (v. 8).

When prophesying God's judgment in Isaiah 30, Isaiah describes the LORD's tongue as a consuming fire (v. 27) and tells the people that they will see the divine arm come down "with raging anger and consuming fire" (v. 30). Not surprisingly, three chapters later, in Isaiah 33, "The sinners in Zion are terrified," asking,

> "Who of us can dwell with the consuming fire? Who of us can dwell with everlasting burning?"
> (Isa. 33.14)

The Israelites knew that they worshipped the God who revealed himself as fire.

There is only one fire: our God who is a consuming fire. Not a literal fire: we do not worship fire as God. Consuming fire is a picture of the fact that God consumes the wicked and judges sin. Refining fire is a picture of his purification of his people.

There is no room in the Scriptures for another, separate fire, reserved for the punishment of the wicked. This fire, too, is to be found in the depths of the LORD, the God described as consuming fire.

In addition, God describes himself as a fire that protects. Through the prophet Zechariah he says:

> "Jerusalem will be a city without walls because of the great number of people and animals in it. And I myself will be a wall of fire around it," declares the LORD, "and I will be its glory within." (Zech. 2.4-5)

The wall of fire keeps wickedness out, and safeguards the holiness within.

4.4 The rich man and Lazarus

The fiery pictures are not limited to the Old Testament. There is also an interesting parable Jesus tells, that some use in order to argue for a hell of on-going pain. It's the parable of the rich man and Lazarus in Luke 16.19-31. The parable tells of a rich man who died and found himself in torment in Hades, and a beggar named Lazarus who died and found himself at Abraham's side. The rich man calls across to Abraham asking him, "Father Abraham, have pity on me and send

Lazarus to dip the tip of his finger in water and cool my tongue, because I am in agony in this fire." (Luke 16.24) Aha! claim some, this proves that hell is a place of on-going pain where the fire does not consume.

One such interpreter is J. I. Packer, who writes, "the fire is a picture not of destruction but of on-going pain" (Packer, 2004, p. 185).

First of all let us note that the rich man is not in *Gehenna*, but in *Hades*. *Hades*, we noted in chapter 2, is more or less synonymous with death, whilst it is *Gehenna* that is often translated as hell and is interpreted as the place of on-going pain.

Whilst I do not agree with Packer's statement above, I affirm the exegetical principles he describes (Packer, 2004, p. 177) one hundred per cent. They are:

1. Passages must be interpreted in context.
2. Biblical writers do not contradict themselves.
3. Keep sight of the immediate point, the persuasive strategy and the intended effect of the author.

So let's apply these principles to the passage in hand. What is the context of the statement about the rich man's fiery agony in this parable? What is the context of this parable? Why did Jesus tell this parable? Why might Luke have chosen to include this parable in his collection of the teachings of Jesus?

The "punchline" of the parable is that people would not be convinced to change their ways even if someone were to rise from the dead. That is the point of the story. The setting of the story is a rich man who ignores the plight of a poor man on his very doorstep. This is a secondary theme.

The immediate context of this parable is that it comes at the end of Luke 16. Luke 14 had the parable of the Great Banquet, Luke 15 has the parables of the Lost Sheep, the Lost Coin and the Lost Son, and Luke 16 begins with the parable of the Shrewd Manager. Thus the parable of the Rich Man and Lazarus comes at the end of a chain of parables.

The parables of the Great Banquet and the Lost Son both begin, "There was once a man..." (in Greek: *anthropos tis*). The parables of the Shrewd Manager and the Rich Man and Lazarus both begin, "There was a rich man..." (in Greek: *anthropos tis en plousios*). The two parables begin identically, and parables in the two preceding chapters begin in a very similar manner.

This helps us considerably in our exegesis. We have a chain of parables, all in the same genre, none of them intended as factual history, all of them, to a greater or lesser degree, including details that make the story more vivid. To argue that the point of the parable of the Rich Man and Lazarus is to give teaching about the fiery nature of hell would be similar to arguing that the point of the parable of the Great Banquet is to give teaching about buying fields, buying oxen and getting married (see Luke 14.18-20).

A fourth exegetical principle we could add to Packer's three is that we should interpret ambiguous texts in the light of unambiguous ones, the opaque in the light of the straightforward, parables in the light of other teachings. As such I take as my starting point the understanding of the concept of "fire" in the rest of Luke, in the rest of the teachings of Jesus, and in other parts of the Bible. Following that process, I see that Luke, Jesus and the Bible state that fire consumes. Therefore I take "consuming fire" to mean "consuming fire," and I exegete this line in a parable in the light of that straightforward meaning.

When I approach this parable of Jesus, then, about the rich man and Lazarus I have the following two points in mind:

1. The overall biblical witness is that God is a fire that consumes and destroys.
2. The purpose of the parable in question was not to give teaching on permanent penal pain, but God's attitude towards the poor and the likelihood of people repenting simply because someone rises from the dead.

Therefore we conclude that in this parable Jesus was using what we might call "poetic licence" in having the rich man conscious of his agony in the fire, and also in enabling him to converse with Abraham from the flames. A parable is not history (past or future). If anyone were inclined to take one part of this story literally (for example, the ongoing pain the rich man experiences in the fire), they at least need to be consistent, and take other parts literally too (for example, that someone in the fire can hold a rational conversation with Abraham, and that the criterion that decides whether you end up with Abraham or in the fire is simply a reversal of this life's fortunes).

A key reference to God and fire in the New Testament is Hebrews 12, which we will look at in the next chapter ("Unshakeable").

5

Unshakeable

At the theophany on Mount Sinai God's voice shook the earth (Exod. 19). God appeared in earthquake, wind and fire. There was noise, there was tumult, there was fear. (Compare 1 Kings 19.12, referred to in section 4.3 above.) At the end of his letter, the author of Hebrews compares and contrasts what can be shaken with what cannot be shaken.

In Matthew 24 Jesus says, "Heaven and earth will pass away, but my words will never pass away." (v. 35). Psalm 102 speaks of "the foundations of the earth" and "the heavens" perishing (v. 25-26). In contrast, "You [the LORD] remain the same" (v. 27). Everything will pass away, except... The key passage is Hebrews 12.22-29. We will quote it in full:

²² But you have come to Mount
Zion, to the city of the living God,
the heavenly Jerusalem. You have
come to thousands upon thousands
of angels in joyful assembly, ²³ to
the church of the firstborn, whose
names are written in heaven. You
have come to God, the Judge of all,
to the spirits of the righteous made
perfect, ²⁴ to Jesus the mediator of a
new covenant, and to the sprinkled
blood that speaks a better word than
the blood of Abel.

²⁵ See to it that you do not refuse him
who speaks. If they did not escape
when they refused him who warned
them on earth, how much less will
we, if we turn away from him who
warns us from heaven? ²⁶ At that time
his voice shook the earth, but now
he has promised, "Once more I will
shake not only the earth but also the
heavens." ²⁷ The words "once more"
indicate the removing of what can
be shaken—that is, created things—
so that what cannot be shaken may
remain.

> [28] Therefore, since we are receiving a kingdom that cannot be shaken, let us be thankful, and so worship God acceptably with reverence and awe, [29] for our "God is a consuming fire". (Heb. 12.22-29)

The following are listed as things that will not be shaken and removed:

> Mount Zion, the city of the living God, the Heavenly Jerusalem (v. 22)
>
> the angels (v. 22)
>
> the full assembly of God's firstborn whose names are written in heaven (v. 23)
>
> God himself (v. 23)
>
> the spirits of good people made perfect (v. 23)
>
> Jesus (v. 24)
>
> the sprinkled blood (v. 24)

Everything else will be shaken and removed. That which can be shaken will be removed. It is that which cannot be shaken that will "remain"

(v. 27). That which can be shaken will cease to exist, consumed in the "consuming fire" which is our God. The only way to escape being shaken, removed and consumed is to be part of the Kingdom of God which is unshakeable (v. 28).

The quotation in verse 29 is from Deuteronomy 4.24 where, back in the Sinai Desert, the Israelites are commanded not to forget the covenant and not to worship false gods:

> Be careful not to forget the covenant
> of the LORD your God that he made
> with you; do not make for yourselves
> an idol in the form of anything the
> LORD your God has forbidden. For
> the LORD your God is a consuming
> fire, a jealous God. (Deut. 4.23-24)

"Shaken" (Heb. 12) and "consumed" (Deut. 4) are two ways of looking at the same activity. That is why the writer of Hebrews quotes Deuteronomy at the end of his passage on shaking. What is this activity? Destruction. The things that are shaken and consumed cease to be. But – and this is the important point in Hebrews 12.27 – not everything will be shaken. Mount Zion, the angels, the full assembly of God's firstborn, God himself, the spirits of good people made perfect, Jesus and the sprinkled blood: these are unshakeable, these remain, they are not consumed.

What is the reason given for Moses' instruction in Deuteronomy? Fear of hell fire? No. Out of fear of God the "consuming fire" who is "a jealous God"? Yes.

The writer to the Hebrews exhorts his readers to worship God "with reverence and awe". Why? Because otherwise God will throw them (us) into hell? No. Because "our God is a consuming fire"? Yes.

There are two significant implications here. Firstly, there is no fire apart from God himself. Some writers and thinkers like to posit another place with the godlike characteristic of eternal-ness, a place of eternal torment, everlasting suffering. But none have eternal life apart from those to whom God chooses to give it. There is no notion in Scripture of an eternal painful life, a shadowy life of everlasting torment and torture. The eternal fire is the Eternal God, the "unquenchable fire" of Matthew 3.12, "the fire [that] is not quenched" of Mark 9.48 and the setting of the "eternal punishment" of Matthew 25.46. There is no separate "place" called "hell" in the Scriptures.

The second significant implication is that the fire consumes. When Moses saw the burning bush (Exod. 3.1-3) he took notice because something strange was happening: the bush was burning but was not being consumed. The exception proves the rule: when something is burned it is consumed by the fire. Those who have not received "a kingdom that cannot be shaken" are consumed by God, the consuming fire. That is, they cease to exist. Annihilation. The end. As if we might be a little unsure of the fact, the Scriptures are careful to state that God is a *consuming* fire. A blazing inferno. What fire does not do is hold an individual in a constant state of conscious torture. If that had been what the biblical writers had intended to communicate, they'd have used different imagery.

6

A refining fire

God, the consuming fire, consumes all that which is not holy. All that which *is* holy he refines. In so doing he is preparing a people who are part of his Kingdom. This is the refining process which the prophet Isaiah describes:

> See, I have refined you, though not
> as silver;
> > I have tested you in the
> > furnace of affliction.
> For my own sake, for my own sake,
> I do this.
> > How can I let myself be
> > defamed?
> > I will not yield my glory to
> > another. (Isa. 48.10-11)

Fire is not mentioned here explicitly, but the refining imagery requires fire. The fire that refines. The same picture is to be found in Psalm 66.10.

The imagery is further developed by the prophet Malachi, who compares the LORD to "a refiner's fire" and "a launderer's soap" (Mal. 3.2). God refines his people (like with fire). He cleanses his people (like with soap).

What are the things that contaminate his people (v. 5)?

Sorcerers (dabbling in the dangerous world of the spirits);

adulterers (those who wreak havoc on the family);

perjurers (those who lie under oath for private gain);

those who defraud labourers of their wages (those who put profits before workers, economic "growth" before equity);

those who oppress the widows and the fatherless (those who use and misuse those who are disadvantaged in society);

> those who deprive the foreigners among you of justice (those who turn away refugees and migrants, and who take advantage of the vulnerable).

These are the things that, according to this passage, matter to God. Not, for example, correct doctrine or belief.

Note how Malachi continues:

> I the LORD do not change. So you, the descendants of Jacob, are not destroyed. (v. 6)

Silver is refined by fire, purified. Wood, on the other hand, is destroyed. "The descendants of Jacob" are silver, refined not destroyed. Borrowing the kingdom language from Hebrews, those who are part of God's Kingdom are refined, not destroyed. The fire consumes. The fire refines. God consumes. God refines. One fire, different results: the results depend on the context.

Does the fire purify or consume me? It looks as though it's important how we experience this fire. In his song, "You have called us chosen" Andy Park includes the following couplets:

> Take our lives as a sacrifice
> Shine in us your holy light.
> Purify our heart's desire,
> Be to us a consuming fire. (Park, 1991)

Park is not praying that he and all who sing his song be annihilated. "Be to us a consuming fire" is paralleled with "Purify our heart's desire." The prayer of this song is that God consume all that is not holy. That is, that God, as in Malachi 3, be a refining fire.

Paul uses similar imagery in his first letter to the followers of Jesus in Corinth as he writes of people building with different materials (gold, silver, precious stones, wood, hay, straw) (1 Cor. 3.12-15). The foundation is Jesus. He is a good and true foundation. Various workers build on that foundation, some better than others. The quality of each person's work will be revealed with fire. Some workmanship will survive, other workmanship will be burnt up. "The Day" – the last day, the Day of Judgment – will test the work each has done. But even if the work is consumed, the builder endures.

At the centre of the book of Revelation is the one seated upon the throne, and the Lamb that looked as if it had been slain (Rev. 5.1-6). It is a book about judgment. This judgment continues until the end of chapter 20, after which John sees "a new heaven and a new earth" (Rev. 21.1). Two Peter says the same thing: the fire that melts everything is followed by the new heavens and new earth (2 Pet. 3.12-13). In both 2 Peter and Revelation "new" means "renewed" not "brand new". We look at the Greek word for "new" in chapter 14. Judgment is important: the new heaven and new earth are sin-free zones. Refining and consuming are key components in God's plan to establish the age to come, which will be free of sin and suffering, pain and death, selfishness, greed and pride.

On coming before God some will enter into his presence, sanctified, purified, refined in the consuming fire, to enjoy eternity, the age to come, with him. Others, on coming before God the consuming fire of judgment will be like wood and stubble, quickly burnt up in the fire. The same fire that refines some consumes others. Not against their will: as Dallas Willard puts it, "I am thoroughly convinced that God will let everyone into heaven who, in his considered opinion, can stand it." (Willard, 1998, p. 330) The consuming fire consumes all that cannot last for ever, all that cannot stand God's heaven. Unless God has clothed us with immortality we cannot last for ever. The consuming fire consumes us and we cease to exist. However, those who are clothed in immortality will be continuously "changed from glory into glory" (Charles Wesley).

7

Immortality

Is the human being immortal? Is part of the human being immortal? Are some human beings immortal? Is part of some human beings immortal? Or is this world all there is, and we eat, drink and are merry for tomorrow we die? In chapter 1 we looked at the tree of life in Genesis 2.8-9 and 3.22-23, and saw that God banished Adam and Eve from the Garden of Eden so that they would not eat of the tree of life and would not live forever. Therefore it is evident that the natural state of humanity is that we are mortal, we die. This is clear from experience: there is only one thing that will certainly happen to anyone and everyone after they are born – they will die, whether they are a daffodil, oak tree, salmon, sparrow, squirrel or human being. Maybe immediately, maybe after a long and fulfilling life.

Michael Greed

What is meant by "death"? Some would argue that it is just the body that dies; that the "soul" is inherently immortal. Those who hold to such a position would say that what died in Genesis 3 was the body: that is, at that point the body became mortal, and even though it did not die immediately, physical death was sooner or later inevitable. However, the notion of an immortal soul comes from Plato (c427-347BC) and Greek philosophy, not from the Hebrew Scriptures. Interpreting Genesis 3 within its own Semitic framework, death means death. Death of the whole being. The story of Genesis 1-3 tells us that mankind is mortal. Yet it also tells us that that does not have to be so, the existence of the tree of life is a glimpse of immortality, a sign that there could be more than just this life.

In the New Testament too, if we are to do justice to the text, death means death. Matthew 10.28 makes it clear (if we were in any doubt) that the death which God brings about is the death of both the body and the soul:

> Do not be afraid of those who kill the body but cannot kill the soul. Rather, be afraid of the One who can destroy both soul and body in hell.

7.1 Body and soul

Men (and women) can kill your body. God is the only one who can kill your soul. What is this "soul"? It is the inner, secret me. It is where I feel, where I think, where I have my passions, my worldview, my depths. When I call on my soul to worship the Lord:

> Praise the LORD, my soul;
>> all my inmost being, praise
>> his holy name.
> Praise the LORD, my soul,
>> and forget not all his
>> benefits—
> who forgives all your sins
>> and heals all your diseases,
> who redeems your life from the pit
>> and crowns you with love
>> and compassion,
> who satisfies your desires with good
> things
>> so that your youth is renewed
>> like the eagle's. (Ps. 103.1-5)

I am calling on all that is within me to praise his holy name. Who am I? What am I? Am I a soul indwelling a body? Am I a body which includes a brain which generates all those things I experience as my "soul"? What is the relationship between someone's soul and body?

This question hit me powerfully when, interestingly, I was reading the story of Mary Queen of Scots. She had been condemned to death. Execution was by decapitation – that is, she would have her head chopped off. The narrative tells how Mary forgave her executioners, was blindfolded, knelt in front of the block, commended her spirit to God – and died. The subject of the narrative then immediately changed. It was no longer "Mary did this" or "that was done to Mary", but "Mary's body was taken away". If Mary's body was taken away, where was Mary? Was she still there, minus body? I tried to imagine the narrative from Mary's point of view. What did she experience the moment after her head was severed from her body? Where was she? The way we speak (and write) implies that the person ceases to exist when they die. Mary was taken to the block. Her head was chopped off. Her body was taken away. Mary herself was no more. Or does the way we use our language suggest that the real me is in fact a soul, and I am simply inhabiting a body? Thus when Mary lost her head did she continue to live but in a disembodied state? Is J. P. Morland right: "I *am* a soul, and I *have* a body" (quoted in Strobel, 2004, p. 261)? Or is the way we use our language just a manner of speech? Or is there something else going on?

Jesus' resurrection was bodily. This is the central fact of the Christian faith. Those who attend a church that recites the Apostles' Creed as part of worship affirm belief in "the resurrection of the body". Just as Jesus' resurrection was bodily, so will ours be. We will examine this further in chapter 9 when we turn to 1 Corinthians 15. Christianity firmly refutes the dualism that suggests that I am made up of two parts, body and soul, that can be disentangled from one another. The two cannot be separated.

If it were just the soul that were immortal, and not the body, the focus of our hope would be an eternal incorporeal existence. The biblical witness, on the other hand, is very much down to earth. God did not create this multi-dimensional universe with all its colours and textures, beauty and variation, glory and wonder simply to prepare disembodied souls for a disembodied afterlife. The vision of the Scriptures is that the whole of creation will be renewed, a new heaven and a new earth, derived from the current heaven and earth but mingled together, which we will inhabit with our new resurrection bodies. Whether the trees and plants and animals that will inhabit the new heaven and earth will be the same as those on this earth I would not like to guess (although it can be fun to conjecture!), but the Bible, affirming matter, affirming flesh, affirming the body, tells us that they will be there.

7.2 Conditional immortality

Immortality – participation in that co-mingled new heaven and new earth – is conditional. Conditional upon being a citizen of that kingdom that cannot be shaken. Conditional upon being part of the assembly of God's firstborn whose names are written in heaven. Conditional upon the work of Jesus, the mediator of a new covenant, and his sprinkled blood (see Heb. 12.22-24). Jesus, as the mediator of the new covenant is the only way, the only means of salvation (see, for example, John 14.5-6). Peter too, in one of his early sermons, states that salvation is found in no one else but Jesus:

> Salvation is found in no one else, for
> there is no other name under heaven
> given to mankind by which we must
> be saved. (Acts 4.12)

Jesus is the only means of salvation.

Who does Jesus save? For whom does he mediate? Scripture is quite clear that Jesus is the only means of salvation, the only gateway into God's age to come. But nowhere does Scripture suggest that a person needs to have heard of Jesus in order to be saved through him. A person who lived chronologically before Jesus, or experientially before Jesus or without the mental faculties to understand Jesus can still be saved through Jesus, as can the person or the community whose path of life has not brought them in touch with the gospel message in an understandable form. Let's not limit our God and his love! Jesus' proclamation was, "Repent, for the Kingdom of Heaven has come near." (Matt. 4.17) It is those who repent, who throw themselves on the mercy of God knowing that they cannot make it on their own, who become citizens of "the city of the living God, the heavenly Jerusalem" (Heb. 12.22).

Does this mean that there is no point in sharing the good news with those who have not heard it? Paul addresses this question in Romans 10. "How, then, can they call on the one they have not believed in? And how can they believe in the one of whom they have not heard?" he asks (Rom. 10.14). Faith, he states, comes by hearing the message (v. 17). Is he stating here that it is only those who have heard the message of Jesus who can believe in God? No. In verse 18, straight after the statement that faith comes from hearing the message, Paul writes, "But I ask: did they not hear? Of course they did," – and goes on to quote Psalm 19.4, Deuteronomy 32.21 and Isaiah 65.1-2 to prove his point that God has provided the means for everyone to hear his voice.

Paul's thrust, then, is not that you cannot experience God's salvation unless you have heard of Jesus. If you cannot experience God's salvation without having heard of Jesus we would be preaching a gospel of salvation by knowledge. Salvation by knowledge is gnosticism, a major heresy against which the early church fought. No! It is God's grace, through faith, that saves us (Eph. 2.8). Paul's point in Romans 10 is that those of us who have experienced the good news have "beautiful feet" (v. 15) as, alongside God's other messenger-witnesses, we share the good news with others.

All God's handiwork proclaims his message. How much more, then, should we who have experienced God's grace share it. The point is not that they will not hear unless we go and proclaim. The point is that, "You will be my witnesses ... to the ends of the earth," (Acts 1.8) and that we have a part to play as God sends his light and truth (Ps. 43.3) into the world.

Immortality, then, is conditional upon throwing oneself upon the mercy of God. Those who do not meet this condition are annihilated. Only God knows the inner workings of each individual and each society, and so there will be surprises. There will be some who are clothed in divine and resplendent immortality enjoying God's new co-mingled heaven and earth, whom we might not expect to see there. There will be others whom we think ought to be there but aren't. But who am I to think such thoughts? Will I be there? Let the prayer of each of us be, "God, have mercy on me, a sinner." (Luke 18.13)

8

Pure delight

This book was conceived about 30 years ago, in the mid-eighties. Brought up in a pretty standard English Baptist church, a hell of eternal torment was part of the picture. I do not have any recollections of specific sermons preaching hellfire, but I knew that the fate of the lost – that is, all humanity bar evangelical Christians – was hell. The picture of hell that was in my mind was one (I regret to say) based on medieval "Christian" art: a lake of fire with people being plunged beneath the fiery waves by devils with pitchforks.

However, I found that the more I reflected on this topic the more I realised that this traditional picture of hell, as handed down by my evangelical tradition, seemed to be in line neither with the straightforward meaning of Scripture nor my understanding of the character of God. Nowhere in Scripture did I find it stated or even suggested that the fate of the majority of humankind would be eternal torment in a lake of fire. What I did find in Scripture was a God who was said to be love, and who revealed himself to Moses as compassionate and gracious, slow to anger, abounding in love and faithfulness, maintaining love to thousands, and forgiving wickedness, rebellion and sin (Exod. 34.6-7).

Exodus 34.7 continues, "Yet he does not leave the guilty unpunished; he punishes the children and their children for the sin of the parents to the third and fourth generation." Does this contradict the compassion and grace? First, let's note that there is nothing about a fiery hell in this punishment. Secondly if we pause we will note that this statement simply reflects reality. My grandfather, for example, was an alcoholic who beat my grandmother. That affected my father. To a lesser extent it has affected me. I trust my own son (fourth generation from my grandfather) is completely free.

Let's return to my spiritual pilgrimage in the 1980s. I began to jot my thoughts down. I did not read other Christian authors on this topic. It was just me and the Bible. Of course it was a great encouragement to me when I found that other, more well-known evangelicals – John Stott and Michael Green, for example – had come to similar positions. I wrote substantial notes at that time, filed them away, and that was it.

8.1 C. S. Lewis and Joy in the 1980s

Although I did not read Stott or Green in the 1980s, one author I did read was C. S. Lewis, and the thoughts I recorded at that time were influenced by Lewis' writings. As we consider immortality, let's go back for a moment to that refining fire that we looked at in chapter 6. Some will approach the consuming fire as gold and silver, clothed in God's righteousness, already being refined in his consuming fire. At the great judgment that refining process will become complete. The "already" and the "not yet" will come together in one. On earth we are already sanctified but, because we are human, we do not live a sanctified life. Before God's throne the process of purification will be completed as, fully sanctified, purified and refined through the fire that consumes all that is not holy, we enter into the very presence of God.

How can I best describe what comes next? Over the last 30 years my understanding of the following particular detail has changed. In the 80s and 90s one aspect of my understanding was timelessness. I understood that while time was a feature of this present age, it would not be a feature of the age to come. That is, the new heaven and the new earth would be outside of time. And so I sought for images and metaphors and ways of understanding eternity as being outside of time. As I did this I found C. S. Lewis to be of great help.

The following section was written in the mid-1980s.

We will not enter the presence of God for an everlasting period of time, for God is outside of time. Rather, the presence of God could better be compared as follows.

Imagine the instant on earth when you were filled with the greatest bliss, the greatest joy, the highest pinnacle of happiness. Just a momentary instant, the memory of a glorious, distant memory. A microsecond when such delight, joy and "immortal longings" welled up from within. Perhaps something akin to what C. S. Lewis describes as "Joy" in his autobiography, "Surprised by Joy".

Lewis's first experiences of Joy were in his childhood and he speaks of one experience in the following way:

> As I stood beside a flowering
> current bush on a summer day
> there suddenly arose in me without
> warning, and as if from a depth

not of years but of centuries, the
memory of that earlier morning at
the Old House when my brother
had brought his toy garden into the
nursery. It is difficult to find words
strong enough for the sensation
which came over me; Milton's
'enormous bliss' of Eden (giving the
full, ancient meaning to 'enormous')
comes somewhere near it. It was a
sensation, of course, of desire; but
desire for what? --- Before I knew
what I desired, the desire itself was
gone, the whole glimpse withdrawn,
the world turned commonplace
again, or only stirred by a longing
for the longing that had just ceased.
It had taken only a moment of time;
and in a certain sense everything
else that had ever happened to me
was insignificant in comparison.
(Lewis, 1955, p.18-20)

On another occasion Joy surprised Lewis when he
was remembering anticipating reading a book he
had just received:

The thought of all the reading before
me, mixed with the coldness and
loneliness of the hillside, the drops

of moisture on every branch, and
the distant murmur of the concealed
town, had produced a longing (yet it
was also a fruition) which had flowed
over from the mind and seemed to
involve the whole body. That walk I
now remembered. It seemed to me
that I had tasted heaven then. If only
such a moment could return! But
what I never realised was that it had
returned – that the remembering of
that walk was itself a new experience
of just the same kind. (Lewis, 1955,
p.135)

I have found these moments of pure delight, these
twinklings of unbounded joy, the desire that
was at one and the same time insatiable and was
itself that which was desired – I have found these
moments in a dance or in a smile, or when singing
or worshipping. I remember one occasion when I
was about 20 when I was helping lead a children's
camp. The whole camp was together singing. A girl
of about 10 was by my side. We were singing, "God
told Noah to build him an arky arky," doing the
actions. At one moment the girl and I exchanged
smiles, and in that moment I experienced that
ecstatic delight that far transcends the physical
environment in which it is situated.

8.2 Glimpses of heaven

Now, 30 or so years later... Lewis and I used the word "moment". A momentary sensation, a moment of ecstatic delight. I still believe these are spontaneous anticipations of the hope that is ours, "thin places" in our experience where heaven stoops down and kisses earth, kisses me on earth. However, I no longer believe they point to a timeless existence in God's age to come. When God created the heavens and the earth in Genesis 1.1-8 he created light on day 1 and a "vault" on day 2. In other words he created space (the vault) and time (light). When we affirm that creation matters and that the new creation will in some way be a renewal of the present creation, we are also affirming space and time. Time, like the rest of creation, will be transformed and renewed. I no longer see eternity as an instant that will always be. To me, that had been the answer to boredom in heaven. My current hope is far more lavish: a transformed time from which any notion of boredom is completely banished.

One of my favourite contemporary songs which has meant a great deal to me contains the line, "Praying for a glimpse of you." (Warren, 2003) In fact I've made it the tag-line on my blog. These moments of pure delight, of enormous bliss, are glimpses of the divine, glimpses of glory, glimpses of the ecstasy and peace God has in store for us, glimpses of heaven. Heaven is this moment – eternally. Not a frozen instant. God's future involves a new heaven and a new earth, co-mingled together. John takes up the story:

> I saw the Holy City, the new Jerusalem, coming down out of heaven from God, prepared as a bride beautifully dressed for her husband. And I heard a loud voice from the throne saying, "Look! God's dwelling place is now among the people, and he will dwell with them. They will be his people, and God himself will be with them and be their God. 'He will wipe every tear from their eyes. There will be no more death' or mourning or crying or pain, for the old order of things has passed away." (Rev. 21.2-4)

Thinking temporal may not help us here, because, as it is put in John Newton's hymn *Amazing Grace*:

> When we've been there ten thousand years
> Bright shining as the sun
> There's no less days to sing his praise
> Than when we first began.

That is because eternity has no beginning and no end. So one way to help us get our minds around eternity might be to imagine that Moment of Joy always being. If we think of eternity in terms of time as we now know it, sooner or later boredom sets in. But boredom is utterly banished from God's new age, his new creation, when He Himself dwells with his people.

If heaven can be described as an eternal moment of pure delight and enormous bliss, can hell be described as an eternal moment of deepest despair, starkest pain and utter forsakenness? Just as the saints experience this moment for eternity (so to speak), do sinners experience their moment for eternity? On the surface this might look like an attractive proposition in that it seems to unite eternal conscious torment with annihilation. But it doesn't work. For the sinners' "experience" to be eternal in the same way as the saints' experience is eternal, the sinner would need in some sense to be alive. But the Scriptures teach that the wages of sin is death (Rom. 6.23). Those outside of Christ die. They do not have life. They do not have some kind of shadowy half-life. They do not have perpetual conscious torment. They die.

9

The resurrection body

In 1 Corinthians 15 Paul discusses the resurrection, resurrection in general and the resurrection body. In verse 20 he exclaims, "But Christ has indeed been raised from the dead, the firstfruits of those who have fallen asleep."

Christ's resurrection body is the prototype or template of all resurrection bodies, the first of its kind, a model or example of future resurrection bodies. So it is fascinating to see what is recorded about Jesus' resurrection body. See, for example, John 21.4-14. Commenting on this passage, Tom Wright (2002, pp. 160-161) writes:

> When Jesus emerged through the locked doors of the upper room, there is a moment where our spines

tingle. 'None of them dared ask, Who are you? They knew it was the master' (v. 12). That is a very, very strange way to put it. It belongs with the other exceedingly strange things that are said in the resurrection accounts. They knew it was him... yet they wanted to ask, and were afraid to.

What did they want to ask? They had been with him night and day for two or three years, and they wanted to ask who he was? I might as well wake up my wife one morning and ask her who she is. If they didn't know him by now they never would.

And yet. The sentence only makes sense if Jesus is, as well as the same, somehow different. No source mentions what he was wearing. No source describes his face. Somehow he has passed through death, and into a strange new world where nobody had ever been before, and nobody has yet been since – though we are firmly and securely promised that we shall join him there eventually. His body was no

longer subject to decay or death.
What might that have been like?

We have no means of knowing.

Jesus was the first. But we are firmly and securely
promised the same kind of resurrection bodies:

> Each in turn: Christ, the firstfruits;
> then, when he comes, those who
> belong to him. (1 Cor. 15.23)

We will not get our resurrection bodies until we
have died:

> What you sow does not come to life
> unless it dies. (v. 36)

The image Paul then goes on to use as he compares
our present body with our resurrection body is
that of a seed and the resulting plant:

> When you sow, you do not plant the
> body that will be, but just a seed,
> perhaps of wheat or of something
> else. (v. 37)

The one is derived from the other, it carries the
same DNA. Whether in terms of appearance,
quality or what isn't specified. But the glimpses
we get from the accounts of the resurrected Jesus

indicate that the resurrection body is the same yet different; the person is recognisable yet they are not the same; the marks of suffering are there (see John 20.27) but the body is not subject to decay.

9.1 Of acorns and oak trees

The oak tree cannot come into existence except from an acorn; it is dependent upon it. But the tree is so much more glorious than the acorn; the flower or stalk of wheat is so much more glorious than the seed. In like manner:

The resurrection body cannot come into existence except from an earthly body – and the earthly body must die for that glorious new body to burst forth.

The resurrection body is a whole lot more glorious than the earthly body, just as an oak tree is a whole lot more glorious than an acorn.

Paul makes a number of contrasts in 1 Corinthians 15 between "the body that is sown" and the resurrection body:

> The former is perishable, the latter is imperishable.

> The former is sown in dishonour, the latter is raised in glory.

> The former is sown in weakness; the
> latter is raised in power.
>
> The former is sown a natural body;
> the latter is raised a spiritual body.
> (v. 42-44)

"Spiritual" here does not mean "un-physical": the "spiritual" body is more physical than the "natural body", as an oak tree is more physical than an acorn, as a body is more physical than a shadow.

Like the contrast between the natural body and the spiritual body, there is a contrast between the ones through whom these bodies come. We have a natural body because we are a son of Adam or a daughter of Eve. In parallel and in contrast with this, it is "the last Adam" who is a life-giving spirit (v. 45). First came the natural, after that the spiritual (v. 46). The first body came from the dust of the ground, the second body comes from heaven, the dwelling place of God (v. 47). Right now we have Adam's characteristics; then we will "bear the image of the heavenly man" (v. 49).

We can receive our imperishable resurrection bodies only if we first have become imperishable beings. In our natural state we are perishable, mortal. But that doesn't have to always be so. For death to die the perishable must become imperishable and the mortal must become immortal. Paul puts it like this in 1 Corinthians 15.50-54, using the image of clothes:

> I declare to you, brothers and sisters, that flesh and blood cannot inherit the kingdom of God, nor does the perishable inherit the imperishable. [51] Listen, I tell you a mystery: We will not all sleep, but we will all be changed— [52] in a flash, in the twinkling of an eye, at the last trumpet. For the trumpet will sound, the dead will be raised imperishable, and we will be changed. [53] For the perishable must clothe itself with the imperishable, and the mortal with immortality. [54] When the perishable has been clothed with the imperishable, and the mortal with immortality, then the saying that is written will come true: "Death has been swallowed up in victory."

While we are no more than flesh and blood we cannot inherit the kingdom of God. But when we have become imperishable (by becoming part of the imperishable, unshakeable kingdom) – that's when the mystery begins to unfold. We will be changed. We will be transformed. We will be radiant. We will shine like stars. "When death dies all things live," sing Michael and Lisa Gungor (2011):

> Like a woman searching and finding love
> Like an ocean buried and bursting forth
> Where it comes flowers grow
> Lions sleep, gravestones roll
> Where death dies all things come alive
> Where it comes water's clean
> Children fed, all believe
> When death dies all things live
> All things live.

9.2 A theology of clothes?

Why do we like to wear clothes? It's not simply to keep warm; not simply to preserve our modesty. We like to dress up, to look good, to feel good. At least, as a middle-aged man I'm a bit more prosaic, but my wife and daughter love their clothes! They choose their garments with care, carefully selecting style and shades of colour. Paul says something similar in 2 Corinthians when he writes, "Meanwhile we groan, longing to be clothed instead with our heavenly dwelling, because when we are clothed, we will not be found naked." (5. 2-3)

Our clothes are like an extension of ourselves; they say something about us. Perhaps our clothes reflect our immortal longings, for the perishable will be clothed with the imperishable and the mortal will be clothed with immortality. When the mortal has become immortal – well, that's the death-blow to death. Where there is mortality death reigns. Where there is immortality death has been swallowed up and is no more. *Thanks be to God, who gives us the victory through our Lord Jesus Christ!* (1 Cor. 15.57)

9.3 Re-embodiment?

Let's get back to our friend David Pawson. He rightly contrasts resurrection with resuscitation. When Jesus raised Lazarus, Lazarus kept the same old body. In contrast, when Jesus rose from the dead he had a new body. "The body that is buried (or cremated, or even totally destroyed) is not the body that will be raised at the resurrection" (Pawson, 1996a, p. 34). Thus far we are in agreement. Pawson then continues:

> God could do either of two things with a disembodied (albeit conscious) spirit. He could annihilate it (since it is mortal) or he could immortalise it (by embodying it again, this time in an immortal body). The big surprise

is that he has chosen to do the latter, not only for the 'righteous' but for the 'wicked' as well. All disembodied spirits are to be re-embodied. This 'general resurrection' is predicted by the prophet Daniel (Dan. 12.2), affirmed by Jesus himself (John 5.29), asserted by the apostle Paul (Acts 24.15) and linked to the last judgment in John's Apocalypse (Rev. 20.5). (1996a, p. 35)

It seems to me that Pawson's argument is economical: since it would be a waste for God to create a new body only to destroy it immediately, Pawson reasons that the resurrection of the "wicked" will continue for ever. The formally disembodied spirit is housed in a new immortal body and therefore cannot die. But we have already noted that immortal, imperishable bodies come from heaven, the dwelling place of God. To argue that an imperishable heavenly body is to be given to the wicked for the purpose of non-stop torment defies the logic of heaven. Heavenly bodies are reserved for those who "inherit the kingdom of God" (1 Cor. 15.50).

We know from John 5.25 and 28 that the dead will hear the voice of Jesus. Therefore we affirm with Pawson that the dead (that is, each of us after we have died) will hear Jesus' voice. Whether that is as a disembodied spirit is open to question. Perhaps we will be re-embodied first, since I am only fully me when I am soul/spirit plus body. What is re-embodiment? As we have already seen, our resurrection bodies are based on and derived from our present bodies. *How* God will do that, I do not know, but *that* he will do it is beyond doubt. Paul writes of a period of "sleep". Since the new creation is a paradigm shift from the present creation perhaps we will all enter it simultaneously, irrespective of the point on the ribbon of time we died in the present age. There are a number of possibilities. What I am critiquing is the assumption that we will at some point after death be "a disembodied (albeit conscious) spirit" (Pawson, 1996a, p. 35).

Yet this is the assumption with which Pawson begins his argument; that we will continue to exist as disembodied, conscious spirits after our bodies have died. I think I am being fair to Pawson if I guess that it is comparable to the evil spirits that Jesus casts out in the Gospels – comparable in its spirit-ness that is, not in its evil-ness. For example, in Mark 5 Jesus casts a legion of evil spirits out of a man. It seems that the last thing these evil spirits want is to be left without a body to live in, so they beg Jesus, "Send us among the pigs; allow us to go into them." (Mark 5.12) Jesus gives them permission and the spirits leave the man and enter the pigs. The pigs in turn rush into the lake and drown.

Pawson's starting point is that a spirit requires a body. I agree with this. However, while Pawson suggests that a spirit can live independently of a body, I would propose that a spirit requires a body in order to live. God breathed the breath of life into Adam in Genesis 2.7. That's what made him come alive. When we die the breath of life leaves us. There wasn't a disembodied spirit floating around that entered Adam when God breathed life into him, and which would then continue to exist after Adam died. The breath, the spirit (they're the same word in Hebrew) was the life.

Therefore I suggest that we will never be disembodied, conscious spirits. I suggest that when we have died we will be re-embodied right away. Some will be re-embodied with immortal, heavenly bodies, others will be re-embodied with temporary, mortal bodies. The former will enjoy the glorious inheritance prepared by God for his family. The latter face annihilation.

Pawson takes four verses, from Daniel, Jesus, Acts and Revelation, to demonstrate that there will be a "general resurrection". Amen! The resurrection of the dead is part of standard Jewish and Christian faith. But that does not mean that God will re-embody disembodied wicked spirits in order that they might suffer torment for ever. No. These verses teach that there will be a general resurrection of the dead where "those who have done what is good will rise to live, and those who have done what is evil will rise to be condemned" (John 5.29).

These verses do not say that the wicked will be immortalised. According to Jesus they will be condemned. I do not find an "economical" argument in the Scriptures, that is, an argument that since disembodied spirits are to be re-embodied, they will therefore live for ever in a state of perpetual torment.

10

The love of God

"How can a God of love throw people into a hell of eternal torment?" is both an emotional and a theological question.

I have made an effort to read the works of those with whom I do not expect to agree. And so, when in 2004 a volume entitled *Hell Under Fire* was published (Morgan & Peterson, 2004), with the tag-line, *Modern Scholarship Reinvents Eternal Punishment*, I purchased it immediately. Has a new argument been discovered, a new exegesis that proves once and for all that "hell" = "eternal conscious torment", and that I am wrong? I turned to the book eagerly.

From the perspective of finding convincing new arguments I was disappointed. The contributors faithfully outlined the arguments of their opponents and then proceeded to argue against them. Sadly (for them) I found the arguments of their opponents a lot more convincing than their own counter-arguments. As such the book was fairly harmless. Until I reached chapter 8. It was a contribution by J. I. Packer entitled, *Universalism: Will Everyone Ultimately Be Saved?* Universalism isn't my theme here, and my position as described in this book is not compatible with universalism. What I am interested in is Packer's study of the love of God in the course of his arguments against universalism.

10.1 Exegetical principles

Packer begins his section by outlining sound exegetical principles. We have already used them in section 4.4 when we were considering the story of the rich man and Lazarus. They are good. They are worth following. I will quote them in full here:

> Now the proper key principles here are, and always will be, that interpretation must be context-specific, author-specific, and focus-specific. That means, first, that passages must be exegeted in terms of the thought-flow of which they are part and not have their

meaning extrapolated beyond the manifest perspectives, limits, and boundaries of that thought-flow; otherwise, we will be reading into them what cannot truly be read out of them. (2) It also means that writers must not be assumed to contradict themselves, but must be respected as knowing their own minds; thus, what they write in one place must be treated as cohering with what they write elsewhere. And it means, finally, that in seeking the writer's meaning, we must never lose sight of the immediate point he is making, the persuasive strategy of which that point is part, and the effect that he shows himself wanting to produce on his readers. The way into the mind, meaning, and message of God the Holy Spirit in the biblical text is always through the mind, meaning, and message of its human writers. (Packer, 2004, p. 177)

To summarise: Packer's three exegetical principles are:

1. Passages must be interpreted in context.
2. Biblical writers do not contradict themselves.

3. Keep sight of the immediate point, the persuasive strategy and the intended effect of the author.

Packer and I are in agreement on this.

On page 182 Packer begins a section on *The Meaning of Eternal Punishment*. He identifies as a "main motive" undergirding universalism "compassionate opposition to the belief that in a good God's ordering of things agony without end could ever be anyone's final destiny" (p. 183). He then proceeds to "explore the love of God as revealed in Jesus" (p. 183).

To do this he begins with the phrase, "eternal punishment," as found in Jesus' story of the sheep and the goats. With regard to the fate of the goats Jesus states:

> Then they will go away to eternal punishment, but the righteous to eternal life. (Matt. 25.46)

Based on Packer's three principles, we would expect him now to comment on the context, examine what Matthew (as the author) writes elsewhere and what Jesus (as the one telling the parable) says elsewhere, and what the point, strategy and intended effect of the passage are.

But that is not what he does. And for the moment neither will we. This is because a whole chapter (ch. 13) is devoted to the topic of sheep, goats and eternal punishment and we will attempt an exegesis of the passage there. What Packer seems to do is read "eternal punishment" as "eternal torment" and then he takes it as his starting point for understanding other passages of Scripture. I, on the other hand, read "eternal punishment" as death.

Let's now focus on Packer and his interpretation of the love of God.

10.2 God's acts of love

When Packer addresses *The Meaning of the Love of God,* he offers a rather weak, not-quite-definition of God's love:

> The love of God set forth in Scripture may be described as an action by God that expresses his goodwill, generosity, and kindness towards the personal subjects who are its direct objects. God's acts of love aim to enrich the loved ones and are calculated to draw out of them the appropriate response of gratitude,

> devotion, and abandonment of all wrong ways. (Packer, 2004, p. 190)

In this definition Packer states that God's love is an action that expresses his goodwill, etc. There are "direct objects" of this action. These "direct objects" become "the loved ones", the recipients of his love. God calculates that his action will make the recipients of his love respond with gratitude and devotion.

If I, as a direct object of God's love, do not respond in gratitude, but rather rebel, has God's calculation failed? Jesus teaches, for example through the parable of the Lost Son in Luke 15.11-32, that the Father's love is unconditional. If I rebel God's calculation has not failed, for the simple reason that God does not calculate. He loves unconditionally.

Who is it that God loves unconditionally? Who are the "direct objects" of the love of God? Packer does not specify. However the most famous verse in the Bible supplies a ready answer: the world (John 3.16). This could lead to universalism, the very position against which Packer is arguing.

Packer's use of the verb "calculated" is particularly surprising. If my "acts of love" towards my wife were simply "calculated to draw out" certain responses from her she wouldn't think much of me. Rather, if my love for her is true, that love will continue whatever she does or does not do.

Therefore we reject Packer's definition of the love of God. The love of God is compassionate, merciful and forgiving (Exod. 34.6-7), patient, kind and unshakable (1 Cor. 13.4-7), indiscriminate, generous and unstinting (Matt. 5.45).

10.3 God is Love

The overt teaching of the Scriptures (Old and New Testaments) is that God is Love. Love is not an adjective or a metaphor; it is a noun. God is Love (1 John 4.8, 16). There are adjectives which describe God (he is holy, just, jealous, etc.); there are metaphors which help us understand what he is like (he is a rock, a shield, a consuming fire, etc.). Love is neither an adjective nor a metaphor: it is what God is.

If we take an adjective that describes God, for example, "God is holy," and turn the sentence around we get, "Holy is God." The new sentence is communicating the same message but in less natural English. If we take a metaphor that describes God, for example, "God is a rock," and turn it around we get, "A rock is God." This is simply not true. A rock has some characteristics that help us understand what God is like: a rock is steadfast and unmoving; God is steadfast and unmoving. But we are not claiming that a rock is God. However, if we take the sentence, "God is Love," and turn it around we get, "Love is God." This is a profound truth. Wherever love is found God is found. Wherever love is present God is present. In saying this we mean of course true love. The Greek word John uses is *agape*. There are some things in the world that may get labelled "love" but which are not love. They may, for example, be lust or infatuation. But where there is love, where there is *agape*, there is God. Where there is God there is love.

Packer, in contrast, seems to redefine the word "is":

> Twice John declares that God is *agape* (1 John 4.8, 16). The logic of the phrase is parallel to that of "God is light" (1 John 1.5) and "our God is a consuming fire" (Heb. 12.29; cf. 12.18; also 6.8; 10.27). "Is" in each of these texts points to the consistent expression of a particular characteristic in God's behaviour towards human beings. (Packer, 2004, p. 191)

"Our God is a consuming fire" is a metaphor, as stated above. As such Packer and I are in agreement:

the metaphor points to a consistent expression of a particular characteristic of God. Light, I suspect, is more like love. It is more than a metaphor. It is more than simply the expression of a particular characteristic. The God of Light, the Light of God, shines in the darkness and the darkness cannot master it (John 1.5).

Packer continues:

> Here the characteristic is love, *agape*. John does not mean that God's character consists of, and his activity expresses, only *agape* to the exclusion of all else, but that all his acts in relation to those who become, and are, Christians ("us," 1 John 4.9-10) are acts of *agape*, one way or another, whatever other aspects of his character they show forth as well. (Packer, 2004, p. 191)

This is where Packer appears to be redefining the word "is". Let me try to paraphrase how I understand what Packer writes: *When John writes that God is Love, he does not mean that God is Love but that the way he relates to Christians is based on agape (love).* However, I suggest that when John writes "is" he means "is". He does not mean "his activities in relation to Christians are based on".

In writing in this manner Packer, it seems to me, is watering down the glorious Scriptural truth of the love of God and doing God a grave disservice. He continues:

> John continues by saying that God's supreme demonstration of this *agape* was sending his Son to be the propitiatory (wrath-quenching) sacrifice for our sins (cf. 2.2), and to become the sustaining source of our new life as God's supernaturally-born children. The particular nuance in all this is well caught in some words from James Montgomery's hymn, "Hail to the Lord's Anointed":
>
>> The tide of time shall never
>> His covenant remove;
>> His Name shall stand forever
>> That Name to us is Love.
>
> It is what God is to Christians specifically that John is highlighting here. (Packer, 2004, p. 191)

"That Name to us is Love." Packer quotes Montgomery's line with approval. But if it is only "to us" that the Name of God is Love, God is not actually Love, and the LORD got it wrong when he told Moses that "his name" was "the compassionate and gracious God" (Exod. 34.5-6, quoted in full below). Is not God love to the rest of humankind – not to mention the rest of creation? Packer states: "God loves all members of the human family in some ways." (p. 191) But this watered-down love is clearly not enough to do anything about their permanent penal pain.

10.4 Is God's love like the tax-collectors'?

In Matthew 5 Jesus says:

> I tell you, love your enemies and pray for those who persecute you, that you may be children of your Father in heaven. He causes his sun to rise on the evil and the good, and sends rain on the righteous and the unrighteous. If you love those who love you, what reward will you get? Are not even the tax collectors doing that? (Matt. 5.44-46)

Jesus commands us to love our enemies. He draws upon the example of God himself who "causes his sun to rise on the evil and the good" – that is, he loves all humankind indiscriminately. Those who love only those who love them in return are no better than tax-collectors – that is, sinners, the lowest of the low. If the statement "God is love" relates only to what God is to Christians, what are the implications? This kind of love, which carefully selects its recipients and is demonstrated only to those who attempt to love God in return (ie. Christians) is on a level with the "love" of tax-collectors and sinners, based on mutual self-interest. I humbly submit that this is not the love of God. This is not the God who is Love. Jesus holds God the Father up as an example of one who loves his enemies, and tells us to do the same. The God who loves his enemies loves them whether or not they love him in return. The God who forgives his enemies forgives them whether or not they repent of their wrongdoing. "Father, forgive them, for they do not know what they are doing." (Luke 23.34)

Packer states that John does not mean that God's character consists of only *agape* to the exclusion of all else, nor that his activity expresses only *agape* to the exclusion of all else. I suggest the opposite: that John *does* mean that God's character consists of only *agape* to the exclusion of all else, and that his every activity *does* express that *agape*.

"God is just" – being just is one of his key characteristics. "God is a rock" – a metaphor indicating that God and rocks have one or more attribute in common. "God is love" – this is a simple statement. God is the source of all love in the world, because he is love. It is his essence. Where there is love, there is God. Where there is God, there is love. It has been said that with regard to the fruit of the Spirit (Gal. 5.22-23) that love is the fruit; the others are simply different flavours of that one fruit: love. If this is true of the fruit of the Spirit of God, how much more is this true of the essence of God himself. "God is just" – this is God's social-action love at work on behalf of those who are not receiving justice; "God is jealous" – this is God's protective love at work for the benefit of his people. And so we could go on.

Christians do experience God's love. We experience God's love in Jesus. We recognise that in the mystery of the cross we are forgiven. Through the death of Jesus, we – in a way we can never fully comprehend – receive life. Jesus is God translated into human form. God the Father is invisible. "Lord, show us the Father!" Well, look at me, says Jesus, and you see the Father (see John 14.8-9). If you want to know the character of God, the essence of God, look at Jesus. Jesus is the ultimate expression of God; his death is the ultimate expression of the love of God, the ultimate expression of the God who is love. Those who are not Christians also experience God's love. "God so loved the world…" that he gave himself in Jesus. The Scriptures do not say "God so loved Christians…" or "God so loved the elect…" The Father sends his rain on the righteous and the unrighteous alike.

10.5 The love of God in the Old Testament

The love of God is not just a New Testament phenomenon. When the apostle John wrote, "God is love" (1 John 4.8, 16) it was towards the end of a lifetime of reflection on Jesus and relationship with God (see Chalke, 2003, pp. 45-46). But how does God reveal himself in the Old Testament? At Sinai Moses asks to see God's glory. God tells him that he will proclaim his name, *Yahweh*, in Moses' presence. And he does:

> Then the LORD[1] came down in the cloud and stood there with him and proclaimed his name, the LORD. And he passed in front of Moses, proclaiming, "the LORD, the LORD, the compassionate and gracious God, slow to anger, abounding in love and faithfulness, maintaining love to thousands, and forgiving wickedness, rebellion and sin. Yet he does not leave the guilty unpunished;

[1] Most English translations of the Bible substitute "the LORD" (in block capitals) for God's name, Yahweh, which is represented in Hebrew by the four letters YHWH.

he punishes the children and their
children for the sin of the parents
to the third and fourth generation.
(Exod. 34.5-7)

The name shows the character. More than that:
the name describes who the person is. The
LORD, "I am," is compassionate, gracious, slow
to anger – the Hebrew can also be translated *long-suffering* – abounding in love and faithfulness.
Forgiving wickedness – while children and
grandchildren will still suffer for the sins of their
parents and grandparents, something we see all
around us and which we accept as part of life. But
since God is love, the punishment fizzles out after
a few generations, while God's love goes on for
ever. The reference to "thousands" could also be
translated, "to thousands of generations". Psalm
136 reiterates this 26 times: "His [the LORD's] love
endures for ever." To borrow a phrase, love wins.

The prophet Hosea captures something of the
fiery passion of God's love in Hosea 11.1-9. God
loves Israel. Not because Israel loves him; in fact
quite the opposite: Israel did not return God's love.
They went the other way. God helped and assisted
Israel, demonstrated love to them – but they did
not realise it. So does God give up and hand Israel
over to destruction? God's passion is aroused, his
compassion makes him act. He does not give up.

He is love: he cannot give up. A man or woman might give up loving a lover who abandons them. But God is not a human being. He never gives up. He calls himself "the Holy One" (v. 9). Holiness and love are not to be held as opposites ("God really wants to love you but because he is holy and you are not, sorry, he can't love you"). Rather God's holiness and love function as one: "Because I am holy and I love you, I will not devastate you but I will have compassion on you and work for your good" (see Hos. 11.8-11).

The love of the God of the Scriptures is passionate and hot-blooded! Jeremy Riddle (2011) expresses it well:

> His love is deep, His love is wide and
> it covers us,
> His love is fierce, His love is strong,
> it is furious,
> His love is sweet, His love is wild,
> And it's waking hearts to life.

Let's give the last word in this chapter to the apostle John himself:

> Dear friends, let us love one another,
> for love comes from God. Everyone
> who loves has been born of God and
> knows God. Whoever does not love

does not know God, because God is love. This is how God showed his love among us: he sent his one and only Son into the world that we might live through him. This is love: not that we loved God, but that he loved us and sent his Son as an atoning sacrifice for our sins. Dear friends, since God so loved us, we also ought to love one another. No one has ever seen God; but if we love one another, God lives in us and his love is made complete in us.

God is love. Whoever lives in love lives in God, and God in them. (1 John 4.7-12, 16)

11

Integrity & torture

Many well-meaning Christians pay lip-service to permanent penal pain, or "eternal torment" as it is more familiarly known. But I suspect that most don't actually believe in it.

BruceG (2009) recounts the story of a man who was listening to a preacher talking about heaven and hell. The man interrupted the preacher and asked whether he truly believed in heaven and hell. "Yes," the preacher replied.

"And you believe that hell is a place of eternal torment, filled with pain and suffering and separation from God forever and ever?"

"Yes, of course."

"If hell is real, as you say you believe it to be, and the pain and misery beyond what we can even imagine, and the length of hell is forever, without end, without hope, with no reprieve, though all of England was strewn with shards of broken glass, if I believed as you say you do, I would crawl across it on my hands and knees, just to be able to save even one soul from entering therein."

But we don't. The Christian's walk does not match his talk.

If I – if you – really were to believe that most people alive today (alongside most people who have ever lived) were heading for a future of eternal conscious torture, permanent penal pain, we would do everything humanly possible and more besides, to try to rescue people from such a fate. We would strive unceasing until we drive ourselves mad trying. But we don't.

A loved-one dies. I do not know whether she has done whatever is needed to secure a place in God's eternal bliss. The stress of not knowing whether or not she is suffering permanent penal pain would be too much to bear – if I really believed in permanent penal pain.

11.1 Bloody tyrants

"Who was the bloodiest tyrant of the 20th century?" asks Matthew White (1999). White compares the track records of Adolf Hitler, Mao Zedong and Iosif Stalin. Do we compare their death toll (Mao 40 million, Hitler 34 million, Stalin 20 million)? Or do we compare their deliberate killings (Hitler 34 million, Stalin 20 million, Mao 10 million?) Or do we confine ourselves to "crimes against humanity" (as opposed to the killing of armed enemy soldiers) (Stalin 20 million, Hitler 15 million, Mao 10 million)? White then goes on to "rank numbers 4 through 10 on the list of the 20th Century's worst killers". The candidates "were responsible for over a million unjust, unnecessary or unnatural deaths by initiating or intensifying war, famine, democide or resettlement, or by allowing people under their control to do so".

What about torture? The warped, depraved mind of man excels itself at finding different ways to inflict the maximum pain on other human beings, and on animals too. Here is one gruesome example, concerning human rights in North Korea (Human Rights Watch, 2013):

> Testimony from North Korean refugees that Human Rights Watch gathered in 2012 indicates that

individuals arrested on criminal or
political charges often face torture by
officials aiming to elicit confessions,
extract bribes and information, and
enforce obedience. Common forms
of torture include sleep deprivation,
beatings with iron rods or sticks,
kicking and slapping, and enforced
sitting or standing for hours.
Detainees are subject to so-called
"pigeon torture" in which they are
forced to cross their arms behind
their back, are handcuffed, hung in
the air tied to a pole, and beaten with
a club.

More details and more examples are available
but I will not elaborate. I trust you get the point.
You probably find the information disturbing,
repellent, inhuman. But Hitler, Stalin, Mao, North
Korean officials – all are sweetness and light
compared to the LORD, if he condemns someone
he has created to permanent penal pain simply
because they was born to a mother who adhered
to the wrong religion, or they had never heard the
name of Jesus, or they rejected their understanding
of the "good news", or they died before having a
chance to respond to the "good news". The multiple
millions of massacres of the world's "greatest"
mass murders fade into insignificance compared

with a Deity who inflicts an eternity of torment upon most of humankind, whom he created in his own image.

Even if we limit the recipients of permanent penal pain to those who live clearly wicked lives or to those who persecute God's people – murders, rapists, terrorists, etc. – a point will come to even the most hardened of us where we cry, "Enough is enough! God, you said, 'An eye for an eye,' Jesus, you said, 'Love your enemies.' Permanent penal pain in response to a few miserable years on earth! At least follow your own laws and limit your retribution!"

This monster, the LORD, then has the audacity to claim to be loving and compassionate, merciful and forgiving? And he expects us to love him? To worship him?

11.2 Challenge to the Church

I would challenge the Church: If you really believed that the fate of all those around you is eternal torture, the likes of which would make Hitler, Stalin, Mao, Pol Pot and all the other mass-murderers and mass-torturers of the world fade into insignificance you would be out there pleading, suffering, imploring, in deepest agony of misery, beseeching, entreating everyone you possibly could to come to Christ. And if you really believed this and also believed that this perpetual torture is the fate not just of those who have rejected Christ but also of all those who, of no fault of their own, happened never to have heard the name of Christ, then you would be unable to endure the emotional agony, the mental misery, the spiritual torture. You'd be crawling over broken glass in order to entreat the last living being to repent and turn to Christ. But no. You are sitting at home enjoying your own spiritual blessings. Or you may be serving God overseas – but if you really believed with all your heart and soul that all those round about you were in imminent danger of a torture chamber of which it could be said, "When you've been there ten thousand years racked with pain and the agony of misery, there's no less time to suffer this torment from when you first began," (whether or not that includes those who have never even heard of Christ) – your ministry would look utterly different from what it does now.

But we don't really believe this. Even those who claim to believe in a hell of eternal torment do not really believe it: just look at their actions.

Well, some do make efforts to put a belief in a hell of eternal torment into practice – with dire results, playing straight into the hands of those who set themselves up against God. Richard

Dawkins visited a "Hell House" run by Pastor Keenan Roberts of Colorado. Dawkins (2006, pp. 359-360) explains, "A Hell House is a place where children are brought, by their parents or their Christian schools, to be scared witless over what might happen to them after they die." Dawkins questioned Roberts about whether the children might have nightmares after one of his performances. Roberts assures Dawkins that he would rather the children understand that Hell is a place that they would absolutely not want to go to. Nightmares are a small price to pay for avoiding Hell. Dawkins summarises, "I suppose that, if you really and truly believed what Pastor Roberts says he believes, you would feel it right to intimidate children too." Dawkins continues his line of argument by giving the testimonies of those who have moved from Christian faith to atheism on account of hell-fire. One testimony begins, "If I think back to my childhood, it's one dominated by fear..." (p. 361) But then (hallelujah!) she was freed from that fear and became an atheist.

The God I know does not manipulate people through fear and what Dawkins calls "religious abuse". The God I know draws us by love – love for those who do not love him, love that we are free to respond to or reject.

A church that claims to believe in permanent penal pain has not only replaced the truth with a lie (although I recognise that many do not do this intentionally), but also lacks integrity. We have integrity when what we claim to believe determines the choices we make in life: when we live according to the words we proclaim, when we practise what we preach, when we walk the talk. If the message to the world is the news that most people are destined for a hell of eternal torment – if this is the talk then the walk can only be "Hell Houses". It can at least be said of Pastor Roberts that he has integrity: his walk matches his talk. If you believe that the future awaiting the bulk of humankind is a hell of eternal torment then you will be perpetually entreating every living being to repent and do whatever it takes to avoid such a terrible fate. That is, if you have any crumb of love and compassion for your fellow human beings. Any other walk does not match the severity of the talk.

If you claim to believe in non-stop conscious torment for the majority of those who have ever lived but are not crawling over broken glass until you can crawl no more, to warn people of this most terrible of fates, then your walk does not match your talk.

Why doesn't the church do this? Because no one really believes it. It is too outrageous, too counter-intuitive, too contrary to what the Scriptures and our conscience tell us about who God is. I would hazard to suggest that even David Pawson, J. I. Packer and those with similar views do not really believe it. An approach like, "Sorry, guys, you're off to a place of permanent penal pain, don't say I didn't warn you," does not resonate as authentic, even when chapter and verse are quoted.

12

The dead will hear

Jesus begins John 5 by healing a sick man. This happened on the Sabbath, and so the religious leaders reprimand the healed man for carrying his mat on the Sabbath. He responds by telling them that the man who healed him told him to. They then (naturally) turn on Jesus himself. Jesus, therefore, in John 5.19-29, explains to them where his authority comes from.

12.1 John 5

This is what he says:

> Very truly I tell you, the Son can do nothing by himself; he can do only what he sees his Father doing, because whatever the Father does

the Son also does. [20] For the Father loves the Son and shows him all he does. Yes, and he will show him even greater works than these, so that you will be amazed. [21] For just as the Father raises the dead and gives them life, even so the Son gives life to whom he is pleased to give it. [22] Moreover, the Father judges no one, but has entrusted all judgment to the Son, [23] that all may honour the Son just as they honour the Father. Whoever does not honour the Son does not honour the Father, who sent him.

[24] Very truly I tell you, whoever hears my word and believes him who sent me has eternal life and will not be judged but has crossed over from death to life. [25] Very truly I tell you, a time is coming and has now come when the dead will hear the voice of the Son of God and those who hear will live. [26] For as the Father has life in himself, so he has granted the Son also to have life in himself. [27] And he has given him authority to judge because he is the Son of Man.

> **28** Do not be amazed at this, for a time
> is coming when all who are in their
> graves will hear his voice **29** and come
> out – those who have done what is
> good will rise to live, and those who
> have done what is evil will rise to be
> condemned. (John 5.19-29)

In *verse 19* Jesus tells them (and us) that he does
only what he sees his Father doing. What does he
see his Father doing? Across history we see him
spreading light and truth, healing, restoration and
reconciliation, forgiveness, joy and peace. And so
Jesus does those very same things. Because Jesus
is God made flesh, he is a kind of "concentration
of divinity". That is, he does what he sees the
Father doing across history, but he does it a lot
more intensively. And so a lot more healing goes
on in Jesus' ministry than elsewhere in history, a
lot more dissemination of light and truth. Jesus
looks across the entire span of history from the
first day until the last and sees what the Father
is doing, and does the same, concentrated into a
three-year span. That, I suggest, may be the reason
why a whole lot more miraculous healings took
place in Jesus' ministry than generally do today.

And so for us, from our perspective, we look at
Jesus and see what God the Father is doing. We
know that God is spreading light, truth, healing,

restoration, reconciliation, forgiveness, joy and peace across history, primarily because that is what we see Jesus doing. We look at Jesus and see God translated into human form. If we want to see what God is doing today, we look and see what Jesus did. That is what God is doing today – but in a more *dilute* form since we don't have the *Divine* walking among us as Jesus did, as Jesus was.

In *verse 20* Jesus pinpoints one particular thing he sees his Father doing: the Father loves. Love is at the heart of the Father-Son relationship. The Father loves the Son. The Son shares with the world what he sees the Father doing. He sees the Father loving. So he, the Son, loves. He loves selflessly and sacrificially.

In *verse 21* Jesus pinpoints a second thing that the Father does: he raises the dead and gives them life. The Son sees the Father raising the dead and giving them life. And so that is what he does. The Son gives life.

12.2 The Son: the Judge

There are two things that Jesus says twice in his speech recorded in John 5.19-29. These are key truths – that's why Jesus repeats them. The first twice-stated truth is in verses 22 and 27:

> Moreover, the Father judges no one,
> but has entrusted all judgment to
> the Son.
>
> And he has given him authority to
> judge because he is the Son of Man.

God the Father has given God the Son authority to judge all humankind because he is the Son of Man, the Messiah. That is, the one who has all the characteristics of God has the authority to judge all humankind because he is also the one who has all the characteristics of a human being. He is Jesus. Without becoming a human being God/ Jesus would have no right, no authority to judge us because he would not have been as we are. Jesus was resilient; he was also vulnerable. And so I can relate to him.

12.3 Hear – hear – live

Verse 24 gives us a simple, elegant sequence of verbs: *hear – believe – live*. It is those who hear the words of Jesus and believe – these are the ones who have eternal life. The sequence of verbs is a little different in the next verse. Verse 25 gives us: *hear – hear – live*: "Very truly I tell you, a time is coming and has now come when the dead will hear the voice of the Son of God and those who hear will live."

Verse 24 had simply said, "Whoever hears." Now verse 25 specifies, "The dead will hear." We stated above that there are two things that Jesus says twice in these verses. The first was that the Father has entrusted all judgment to the Son. We now come to the second twice repeated statement: the dead will hear the voice of Jesus.

> Very truly I tell you, a time is coming and has now come when the dead will hear the voice of the Son of God and those who hear will live. (v. 25)

> Do not be amazed at this, for a time is coming when all who are in their graves will hear his voice. (v. 28)

Both verses carry emphasis markers. Verse 25 begins with what the King James Version famously translated as *Verily, verily*. Verse 28 anticipates amazement and disbelief. All who are in the grave will hear the voice of Jesus. In other words, Jesus recognises that we might find this hard to believe. So he emphasises that it is true. No one is without excuse. Jesus is clear that you don't have to have heard his physical name in order to hear his voice and rise to life. Everyone hears the voice of Jesus.

The tense of the verb is noteworthy. "The dead will hear his voice." The word "dead" implies past tense.

Dying is something you do after living, not before. But the verb is in the future tense: "will hear". In choosing to phrase himself in this manner – and choosing to do it twice! – Jesus is emphasising his belief in life after death for all, good and evil alike. When will this happen? Verse 25 begins, "A time is coming and has now come." It's happening now! It's happening now?

At the end of chapter 9 we discussed the "general resurrection" – that is, the time when all are raised to life. Traditional Jewish belief put this at the end of time – see for example Martha's reply to Jesus in John 11 when Jesus tells her that her brother will be raised to life. Jesus says to her in John 11.23, "Your brother will rise again." Yes, she says, "I know he will rise again in the resurrection at the last day." This then elicits Jesus' famous statement, "I am the resurrection and the life. The one who believes in me will live, even though they die; and whoever lives by believing in me will never die."

In Jesus the age to come has gate-crashed the present age. In Jesus features of the age to come can be found in this age. So when, in John 5.25, Jesus says that the time "has now come" he is pointing to himself. *Look,* he is saying, *I am the inauguration of the age to come; the general resurrection begins with me. I am the resurrection.*

The Greek of John 5.25 has the same verb twice, as reflected in the NIV translation: "the dead will *hear*" "those who *hear* will live". What does this mean? First of all, we note that in the parallel sequence of verbs in verse 24 we have: *hear – believe – live*. Secondly we note the immediate context which indicates that there are probably two different nuances of the word "hear" here. Thirdly, when we get to verse 29 we see that some of those who hear his voice "live" while others are "condemned". Therefore the New Living Translation, for example, translates the second "hear" as, "Those who listen will live." Listening means taking in, internalizing what we have heard, believing. This understanding makes good sense and fits in with the overall context. Our sequence of verbs, then, is: *hear – listen – live*.

This is contrasted in verse 29 with another sequence: *hear – don't-listen – condemned*. Before we leave these verses let's note who lives and who is condemned. In verse 29 it is "those who have done what is good" who rise to live and "those who have done what is evil" who will rise to be condemned. This is reminiscent of the story of the sheep and the goats in Matthew 25 (see ch. 13) where judgment is based solely on what the sheep and goats did and didn't do. This doesn't contradict listening and believing. It simply demonstrates that listening and believing are action verbs. Our listening and believing is seen in our actions.

Finally, a word on that word, "hear". No one need wait until they are dead before they hear. Everyone has a chance to hear before they die. Jesus speaks in many different ways. A handful of people in first century Palestine heard him while he was a human being, and of those who heard, some listened and lived. Some of us hear him through his written word. And if we listen, we live. Many more hear him through the testimony of nature, creation and conscience. This is all the voice of Jesus: and if they listen they live.

> The heavens declare the glory of God,
>> the skies proclaim the work of his hands.
> Day after day they pour forth speech,
>> night after night they reveal knowledge. (Ps. 19.1-2)

13

Eternal punishment

We noted in chapter 10 that the parable of the sheep and the goats in Matthew 25 is Packer's starting point in his interpretation of "eternal punishment" as "permanent penal pain". Let's now look at that parable. It comes at the conclusion of Jesus' fifth and final discourse in Matthew's Gospel. (Compare Matt. 26.1, "When Jesus had finished saying all these things," with Matt. 7.28, "When Jesus had finished saying these things," – marking the end of the first discourse.)

13.1 The sheep and the goats

The so-called parable of the sheep and the goats is not so much a parable as a narrative about judgment. It's not about sheep and goats either. Sheep and goats are brought in as a simile, "As a shepherd separates the sheep from the goats," (v. 32) which is then continued as a metaphor in verse 33: "He will put the sheep on his right and the goats on his left."

The scene is set: "When the Son of Man comes in his glory, and all the angels with him." (v. 31) All nations, all peoples will be gathered before him, and the Son of Man, who is then identified with the King, divides them into two groups. The "labels" of these two groups are *sheep* and *goats* – but that's all they are, mere labels. The sheep are called "those on his right" and "the righteous". The goats are called "those on his left" and "they". That is, while the first group are identified as "the righteous" the second group receive no such identifier, good or bad. For this reason it is often easier to use the labels *sheep* and *goats* when referring to these two groups. To label them *the righteous* and *the others* is rather unwieldy.

The first group, those on his right, the righteous, gave the King something to eat when he was hungry, gave him a drink when he was thirsty, invited him into their homes when he was a stranger, gave him clothes when he was naked, looked after him when he was ill and visited him when he was in prison. They are invited to "take your inheritance, the kingdom prepared for you since the creation of the world." (v. 34)

The second group, the goats, are those who failed to give the King something to eat, who failed to give him something to drink, who failed to invite him in, who failed to clothe him, who failed to visit him. They are told: "Depart from me, you who are cursed, into the eternal fire prepared for the devil and his angels." (v. 41) This is later summarised as "eternal punishment" (v. 46), while the destination of the first group, the righteous, is summarised as "eternal life" (v. 46).

The only difference between the sheep and the goats according to this narrative is what they did and didn't do. The sheep receive eternal life because they fed the hungry, etc. The goats are sent off to eternal punishment because they did not feed the hungry, etc. Does Paul disagree with Jesus, then, when he teaches justification by faith? For example, in Ephesians 2.8-9 he writes, "For it is by grace you have been saved, through faith – and this is not from yourselves, it is the gift of God – not by works, so that no one can boast," and in Romans 3.28 he writes, "For we maintain that a person is justified by faith apart from the works of the law." What matters: feeding the hungry or faith?

We will see that it is the sheep who both give and receive grace, while it is the goats who are trying to earn their salvation through good works. But first let's take a look at the structure of this parable. The scene is set in verses 31-33: the King is on his throne; he separates the sheep from the goats.

> v. 34-36: the King welcomes the righteous because they fed him when he was hungry, etc.

> v. 37-39: the righteous are surprised. They protest that they were never aware of feeding the King when he was hungry, etc.

> v. 40: the King responds, "Truly I tell you, whatever you did for one of the least of these brothers and sisters of mine, you did for me."

> v. 41-43: the King banishes "those on his left" because they did not feed him when he was hungry, etc.

> v. 44: they are surprised. They protest that they never saw the King hungry, etc.

> v. 45: the King responds, "Truly I tell you, whatever you did not do for one of the least of these, you did not do for me."

> v. 46: these are sent off to eternal
> punishment, while the righteous go
> to eternal life.

13.2 Surprise!

Note the surprise! This is a key (and surprising) element to this story. Neither the sheep nor the goats expected the verdict which they received. In telling the parable this way Jesus is telling his listeners, *Expect surprises! Those of you who think you're righteous may be cursed. Those of you who just went about doing good to other people, you are the ones who are truly righteous.*

The sheep protest. "Lord, when did we see you hungry and feed you? ..." They were blissfully unaware that they had been serving the King. They did not feed the hungry or clothe the naked for what they could get out of it. They showered compassion on their fellow-human-beings simply because their hearts were full of compassion. They, as it were, couldn't help themselves. They lived a life of practical love – and found that those whom they fed, clothed, visited, etc. were the King himself.

They didn't think in terms of being "in" or "out", and they were "in".

The goats also protest. "Lord, when did we see you hungry or thirsty? …" They thought they were OK, that they were acceptable to the King. Those who were banished into "the eternal fire prepared for the devil and his angels" were those who thought they had it all sewn up with God. They didn't realise that what mattered was feeding the hungry, giving drinks to the thirsty, welcoming strangers, clothing the naked, caring for the sick and visiting the imprisoned. These are the ones who receive "eternal punishment". Irrespective of the nature of this eternal punishment, it is crucially important to see who are the ones who receive it. It is not those who fail to accept Jesus as Saviour. It is not those who fail to get baptised, or are not a member of the church, or who are not born again. It is not those who fail to give assent to certain doctrines or statements of faith. No, those who go away to eternal punishment in this narrative of Jesus are those who fail to show practical love and compassion to their fellow-humans.

They thought they were "in" but they were "out".

This answers the question posed earlier about feeding the hungry vs faith: which saves us? The two cannot be separated. The sheep fed the hungry not out of a sense of duty or legalism. They didn't do it so that they could boast about it or receive a reward. They did it because their hearts told them it was the right thing to do. The sheep demonstrate grace and receive grace. It was the goats who were trying to earn their salvation through good works. They thought they had done the right things: they were surprised to find they hadn't. Paul, then, is absolutely right: we are saved by grace through faith. We are justified on the basis of our faith, not because we have followed the law. That is, we are justified because our hearts are right not because we are doing the "right" things simply so that we can be justified. This is evidenced by the fact that we feed the hungry and have practical compassion on all whom God has made. Jesus is also absolutely right.

13.3 A rabbit trail

There are those, like J. I. Packer, who will cite this narrative as evidence for permanent penal pain in the afterlife for those who are not Christians. But this is not what the story teaches. What it teaches is that those who do not live a life of practical love will receive "eternal punishment", while those who do live a life of practical love will inherit eternal life. The marked element of surprise in the narrative warns us that those who think they are going to inherit eternal life may get eternal punishment, while those who do not think in terms of getting through the final judgment – they are the ones who will inherit eternal life.

What Packer seems to do in his interpretation of this passage is to break his own rules of exegesis. He takes the phrase "eternal punishment" from this story (with no comment on context, author or intent) and scoots over to Revelation 20. There he finds the following two verses:

> And the devil, who deceived them, was thrown into the lake of burning sulphur, where the beast and the false prophet had been thrown. They will be tormented day and night for ever and ever. (v. 10)

> Anyone whose name was not found written in the book of life was thrown into the lake of fire. (v. 15)

Revelation was not written by Matthew. Revelation 20 does not cite the words of Jesus. Matthew 25 is a narrative while Revelation 20 is the climax of an apocalyptic vision. But despite his own excellent principles of exegesis, Packer takes these two verses from Revelation and uses them to determine his conclusion with regard to what Jesus (and Matthew) meant in the parable of the sheep and the goats: Packer writes, "Eternal punishment" in Matthew 25.46 "affirms permanent penal pain for some after death" (Packer, 2004, p. 183).

If Packer has considered the overall thought-flow, the overall context of the writers and the immediate point in the specific context (the three principles of exegesis quoted in ch. 10) he does not share this wisdom. We simply leap to the conclusion that "eternal punishment" in Matthew 25.46 "affirms permanent penal pain for some after death". Packer has read into the parable that which cannot be read out of it, he has caused Matthew and Jesus to contradict themselves, and he has lost sight of the intended meaning of the story.

But, now that Packer has this premise, this "conclusion" already reached on the basis of his shaky exegesis of Matthew 25, he can approach other biblical texts and read permanent penal pain back into them – for example the texts about Gehenna considered earlier.

13.4 Eternal punishment

But to return to the text, what the King says in verse 41 is, "Depart from me, you who are cursed, into the eternal fire prepared for the devil and his angels." The fire is eternal. That of course is because it is our God who is a consuming fire. It was "prepared for" (that is, this aspect of the nature of God exists because of) not human beings but "the devil and his angels". It was not prepared for human beings, and it gives the King no joy in sending some of his created mortals there.

Then in verse 46 this fate is summarised as "eternal punishment".

Eternal in the sense that a point has been reached where there are no more second chances. In order to share in the life of the age to come our mortality needs to be clothed in immortality, we need to eat of the tree of life. Without that, we are mortal. Death is eternal, in that we cease to exist at that point.

Punishment in the sense that we are missing out on God's glorious future, missing out on "the kingdom prepared … since the creation of the world".

Is the King being unfair in meting out this eternal punishment? The key characteristic of the "kingdom prepared … since the creation of the world" as seen in this story is practical compassion. If I have failed to show practical compassion in this present age I would feel distinctly ill-at-ease and not-at-home in God's kingdom where all citizens are spontaneously and continuously showing practical compassion to one another out of the love that is in their hearts through their connection with divine love. In that the goats have already decided against that in this world, they have already chosen their fate in the next.

Seen in the context of this story told by Jesus in Matthew 25, eternal punishment, then, is not, as Packer suggests, "a divine penal infliction that is ultimate in the same sense in which eternal life is ultimate – prima facie, therefore everlasting and unending" (Packer, 2004, p183). The "penal infliction" that Packer conjectures is a form of everlasting life, in that he pictures the cursed continuing to live for ever, and while doing so they suffer torment and torture. What Jesus states is that the punishment is eternal. No torment or torture is mentioned, no penal pain or infliction; simply punishment. Since they are missing out on eternal life the punishment is eternal.

But the home of the King, the kingdom prepared since the creation of the world, the age to come, is one of selflessness, self-giving, compassion and love, and those who failed to display such characteristics in the present age would never be able to make it their home. And so, with tears in his eyes, the King allows them to go their way. They have rejected the way of love and are consumed in the consuming fire, which is our God. The punishment is instantaneous and complete – and eternal.

14

Eternal life

When we looked at the Greek word *aionios* (eternal) in chapter 3 we began to look at the nature of eternal life. Now, as we begin to draw this book to a close we will pull together a number of strands relating to eternal life.

In the story of the sheep and the goats the sheep are welcomed into their "inheritance, the kingdom prepared for you since the creation of the world". (Matt. 25.34). At the end of the story this is summarised as "eternal life" (v. 46), and it was part of God's plan when he created the heavens and the earth.

The central focus of Jesus' teaching was the Kingdom of Heaven, which, he declared, had "come near" (Matt. 4.17). The thrust of many of the parables of the Kingdom is that the Kingdom begins small and negligible, but then grows. An example of this is the parable of the mustard seed: "The kingdom of heaven is like a mustard seed, which a man took and planted in his field. Though it is the smallest of all seeds, yet when it grows, it is the largest of garden plants and becomes a tree, so that the birds come and perch in its branches." (Matt. 13.31-32)

This is reminiscent of Paul's teaching in 1 Corinthians 15 about our resurrection bodies. Paul writes of sowing "a seed, perhaps of wheat" (v. 37). In chapter 9 I preferred the picture of the acorn and oak tree. The picture is the same: the mustard seed that becomes a large tree, the grain of wheat that becomes a full ear of wheat, the acorn that becomes an oak tree. This isn't limited to plant life; the same can be said of animals, including humans. Many years ago I was a baby; before that I was a foetus the size of an ear of corn. Before that I didn't exist. But now I do. The miraculous truth is that God created the world in such a way that new life is continuously being engendered, and having been engendered it grows.

In the same way the age to come is engendered by this age. Paul uses this very same picture in Romans 8.22 where he writes, "The whole creation has been groaning as in the pains of childbirth right up to the present time."

14.1 Two kinds of new

When John declares that he sees "a new heaven and a new earth" (Rev. 21.1) he sees a *kainos* heaven and a *kainos* earth – not a *neos* heaven and *neos* earth. In Greek there are two words that are translated, "new". There is *neos* which means "new" in the sense of "not previously existent" or "brand new", and there is *kainos* which is more qualitative and could be translated "renewed" – for example the new (*kainos*) covenant which is derived from the first covenant.

The new creation, then, is based on, derived from, this creation, in the same way perhaps that an oak is derived from an acorn, a mustard tree from a mustard seed, or a man or woman from their parents. The present creation gives birth to the new creation.

14.2 God with us

Eternal life is participation in God's new creation. It will be more real than this creation, not less so. No disembodied spirits will be there. In fact our current bodies might seem like disembodied spirits in comparison to the new immortal bodies in which we will be clothed. There will be both continuity and discontinuity with the present age. That is, some features will be similar and other features will be different. We can only imagine what it will be like. However one thing we know for sure: there will be no sin and no effects of sin. All that is sinful in this creation will have been judged, and will not be present in the new creation.

In the present age heaven and earth are separate. In the coming age they will mingle and merge. The exclamation in Revelation 21.3 is, "Look! God's dwelling-place is now among the people, and he will dwell with them." The biblical vision and promise has always been "God with us". Not "us with God" but "God with us". That is fulfilled *par excellence* in the new heaven and earth where God comes down to dwell among his people, here on earth – that is, on the new earth which is comingled and interpenetrated with the new heaven.

What other characteristics of the new heaven-earth are given? God "will wipe every tear from their eyes. There will be no more death or mourning or crying or pain" (v. 3). The wiping away of every tear from our eyes suggests a healing process. As we transition from this age to the age to come God is at work in us in a way we never experienced or even imagined before. The healing he brings is full and complete as sin and suffering are no more.

As I write this section my ankle is injured. According to my physiotherapist I got over-enthusiastic when out running, and strained a tendon. As I ran down that hill I felt as though I were flying, stretching one leg in front of the other, the ground almost not there. When God has wiped away the tears from our eyes and brought an end to suffering there will be no "over-enthusiastic". We will run, we will fly, we will soar together, and we will rest peacefully in the Kingdom of *Shalom*.

14.3 Ancient prophecies

The ancient prophecies of Isaiah speak of rivers flowing through the desert (for example, Isa. 41.17-20). The desert is tough, it's dry and barren. It was when he was in the desert that David prayed, "You, God, are my God, earnestly I seek you; I thirst for you, my whole being longs for you, in a dry and parched land where there is no water." (Ps. 63.1) The river brings life. The river is life. Perhaps our experience in this world can be compared to a river running through the desert. There is life, there is joy, God is with us, there is a sense of bubbling freedom. But it is constrained. The desert is all around us. But the river that now runs through the desert runs to the sea.

Let's now turn to the sea. Another ancient prophecy of Isaiah speaks of a righteous judge coming from "the stump of Jesse" (Isa. 11.1) who will slay the wicked. Under his rule the lion will lie down with the lamb, the nations will rally to him and "the earth will be filled with the knowledge of the LORD as the waters cover the sea" (v. 9). In what way do the waters cover the sea? The waters are the sea. Where does that seawater come from? In part it comes from all those rivers flowing through the desert. The route of the river is always to the sea, and the waters of the rivers become part of the waters of the sea. Our suffering, our pilgrimage, is not in vain. The prophet's statement is:

> the earth – full of the knowledge of God
>
> the sea – full of water

In the same way that our rivers running through the desert become part of the Ocean of God, so our gropings and glimpses of the knowledge of God become full and complete as the earth becomes saturated with the knowledge and glory of God, as God takes up his residence upon the earth.

14.4 Knowing God

The phrase "eternal life" (in Greek: *zoe aionios*) occurs 43 times in the Greek New Testament. Most of these occurrences speak of *inheriting* eternal life or *receiving* eternal life or *having* eternal life. In fact only one of these 43 instances states what eternal life is. In John 17.3 Jesus prays, "Now this is eternal life: that they know you, the only true God, and Jesus Christ, whom you have sent." Quite simple really: eternal life is knowing God, and knowing Jesus Christ whom he sent. All the rest, the inheriting and receiving and having, our sharing in God's new creation in his new heaven-earth: it all comes down to knowing God. Not knowing *about* God, but knowing him, experiencing him, relating to him, being full of his love and compassion.

Knowing is a two-way process: we know God; he knows us. Jesus warns us in this regard that there are those who think God knows them, but he doesn't: "Many will say to me on that day, 'Lord, Lord, did we not prophesy in your name and in your name drive out demons and in your name perform many miracles?' Then I will tell them plainly," says Jesus, "I never knew you. Away from me, you evildoers!" (Matt. 7.22-23) This is the same warning as is found in the story of the sheep and the goats (see chapter 13): the goats thought they knew the King, but they did not.

Eternal life: knowing and being known. God himself, Father, Son and Holy Spirit, is the perfect community, sharing perfect love, knowing each other perfectly. We are invited to join that community. William Barry (quoted in Chua, 2010, p. 5) suggests, "It is as if the three Persons said to one another, 'Our community is so good: why don't we create a universe where we can invite others to share our community?'" Then we will know fully, even as we are fully known (1 Cor. 13.12).

15

Fear the Lord

Eternal life, then, is knowing God. In the new heaven-earth he comes to dwell with us and we get to know him better and better moment by moment. In a way it's like Eden where God walked in the garden chatting with Adam and Eve, but now we have eaten of the tree of life; in fact we continuously eat of the tree of life, for it bears fruit every month (Rev. 22.2).

15.1 Summary

However, we saw in chapter 1 that when Adam and Eve ate the fruit of the tree of the knowledge of good and evil, God's response was to forbid access to the tree of life. As the story unfolded we saw that God does in the end give some mortals access to the tree of life, and those who eat live. We humans are mortal, we die, unless we are amongst those who eat the fruit of the tree of life.

We then looked at the Greek and Hebrew words translated as "hell", "world of the dead", etc. (ch. 2). We noted that the concept of permanent penal pain is absent from all of them. We then showed that what is conceptualised as "hell" is an activity and manifestation of God himself.

We then moved from hell to heaven, and saw that they are not opposites (ch. 3). Heaven, the place where God lives, is contrasted with earth, the place where humans live. Next we followed the equation of God with fire throughout the Scriptures (ch. 4). This brought us to our key passage in Hebrews 12 where what is shaken and destroyed is contrasted with what is unshakeable and lasts for ever (ch. 5). Concluding the section on God and fire, we then looked at another attribute of fire, that is its refining nature, and noted that while fire consumes that which is not holy, it purifies that which is holy (ch. 6).

Is the human being immortal? This is the question we addressed in chapter 7. Noting that theories of the immortality of the soul come from Plato and not from the Scriptures, we examined the nature of the soul, and affirmed that when biblical writers say "death" they mean "death". They do not mean torture. Some people will cease to exist, but none will experience never-ending torment. We then wondered what the pure delight of the age to come might be like (ch. 8).

Moving on to the nature of the resurrection body (ch. 9), we noted that there is one instance where there is a resurrection body in the present age: the resurrected Jesus. His resurrection body was the same but different, recognizable yet unrecognizable. We suggested that the relationship between our present body and our future body might be something like the difference between an acorn and an oak tree. We also suggested that our use of clothes may reflect our immortal longings.

Next we examined what it means for God to be love (ch. 10). Rejecting J. I. Packer's definition of God's love, we argued that love is God's defining characteristic, a passionate, hot-blooded love. In chapter 11 we dared to suggest that those who claim to believe in a hell of permanent torture actually don't, since their walk does not match their talk.

We then turned to one of Jesus' great discourses, John 5, and examined the relationship between hearing, listening/believing and living, and to the climax of Jesus' teaching in Matthew, Matthew 25, to get greater insights into the nature of eternal life and eternal punishment (ch. 13). Eternal life is given by Jesus to those whose actions show that they have taken his message to heart. Eternal punishment is a big surprise: those who thought they were OK were sent away to eternal punishment, while those who received eternal life were simply acting spontaneously out of the love in their hearts.

Chapter 14 took a closer look at eternal life, and noting that the Greek word for new does not mean "brand new" but "renewed" we saw how the present age gives birth to the age to come. Finally, we saw that Jesus defines eternal life as simply *knowing God.*

15.2 A response

To round off this book we will examine what an appropriate response is to our God who is a consuming fire. It is in Deuteronomy 4 where God is first called a "consuming fire":

> The LORD your God is a consuming fire. (v. 24)

The context is a speech by Moses on the importance of obedience. Moses begins:

> Now, Israel, hear the decrees and
> laws I am about to teach you. Follow
> them so that you may live and may
> go in and take possession of the land
> the LORD, the God of your ancestors,
> is giving you. (v. 1)

Moses (and the LORD) know the people well. He
knows that they will be sloppy in their obedience.
The LORD still knows us well and we are still
sloppy in our obedience. Moses exhorts the people
to obedience in different turns of phrase throughout
the first part of his speech. He comments on the
temptations to idol worship and exhorts them not
to make idols in the form of men, women, animals,
birds, fish, the sun, the moon and the stars (v. 16-
19). Then he summarises:

> Do not make for yourselves an idol
> in the form of anything the LORD
> your God has forbidden. For the
> LORD your God is a consuming fire,
> a jealous God. (v. 23-24)

The LORD is a consuming fire, therefore worship
only him. The LORD is a jealous God who will
not tolerate any rivals to his affections, therefore
worship only him. The LORD is a consuming fire,
a jealous God, so fear him.

But even if you do blow it and go astray the LORD, the consuming fire, will not consume you completely. "If … you seek the LORD your God, you will find him if you seek him with all your heart and with all your soul." (v. 29) There is always room to return to the Lord, since:

> The LORD your God is a merciful God; he will not abandon or destroy you or forget the covenant with your ancestors, which he confirmed to them by oath. (v. 31)

The theme of fire returns in verse 36:

> From heaven he made you hear his voice to discipline you. On earth he showed you his great fire, and you heard his words from out of the fire.

where the point of God's communication is not punishment but "discipline", and where the theme of fire is juxtaposed with God's love again: verse 37 begins, "Because he loved your ancestors…"

In Hebrews 12 the author is exhorting his readers and listeners to press on and not give up. "Let us run with perseverance the race marked out for us," he says in verse 1. There is a close parallel between Deuteronomy 4 and Hebrews 12: *press on, don't give up*, both authors urge. *Hard times will come*, both authors warn, *but see them as discipline not punishment.* You will mess things up, but that doesn't mean it's all over.

At Hebrews 12.18 the exodus narrative of Deuteronomy comes from the background into the foreground. Mount Sinai is compared to Mount Zion. You, the reader of the letter, have not come to Mount Sinai with its burning fire and billows of smoke, but you have come to Mount Zion, to the city of the living God, the heavenly Jerusalem. Mount Zion is incomparably better than Mount Sinai, continues the author of Hebrews, so we have all the more reason to obey:

> See to it that you do not refuse him who speaks. If they did not escape when they refused him who warned them on earth, how much less will we, if we turn away from him who warns us from heaven? (Heb. 12.25)

God will shake the earth and the heavens. What can be destroyed will be destroyed in this shaking. And what cannot be destroyed will endure. The conclusion:

> Therefore, since we are receiving a kingdom that cannot be shaken, let us be thankful, and so worship God

> acceptably with reverence and awe,
> for our "God is a consuming fire."
> (Heb. 12.28-29)

God is a consuming fire, and yet he has given us a kingdom that cannot be shaken, that will not be consumed. Therefore let us:

> Be thankful.

> Worship him with reverence and awe.

This is our only true response.

References

Bell, R. (2011) *Love wins*, London: HarperCollins.

BruceG (2009) *The Broken Glass Test.* Available at <http://bibleforums.org/showthread.php/190845-The-broken-glass-test>. [Accessed 25 June 2014]

Chalke, S. (2003) *The Lost Message of Jesus*, Grand Rapids, Michigan: Zondervan.

Chua, H.C. (2010) *Perichoresis and Missio Dei: Implications of a Trinitarian View of Personhood for Missionary Practice.* Available from: <http://www.scribd.com/doc/62278399/A-Trinity-and-Mission-H-C-Chua> [Accessed 22 August 2012].

Dawkins, R. (2006) *The God Delusion*, London: Black Swan.

Goodrick, E.W. & Kohlenberger III, J.R., (1990) *The NIV Exhaustive Concordance*, London, Sydney, Aukland, Toronto: Hodder & Stoughton.

Gungor, M. & Gungor, L. (2011) "When Death Dies", from the album *Ghosts upon the Earth*, Atlanta, GA: Brash Music. Available from <http://gungormusic. com> [Accessed 27 December 2011].

Human Rights Watch (2013) in *World Report 2013*. Available from: <http://www.hrw.org/world-report/2013/country-chapters/north-korea> [Accessed 25 June 2014].

Lewis, C. S. (1955) *Surprised by Joy*, Glasgow: Fount Paperbacks.

Morgan C.W. & Peterson R.A., editors (2004) *Hell under fire: Modern Scholarship Reinvents Eternal Punishment*, Zondervan Publishing House.

Newton, J. *Amazing Grace*.

Nowels R. and Shipley E. (1987) *Heaven is a place on earth*, MCA Records. A number 1 hit in many countries by Belinda Carlisle in 1987. Available at: <http://youtu.be/P-WP6POdTgY> [Accessed 16 June 2014].

Packer, J. I. (2004) "Universalism: Will Everyone Ultimately Be Saved" in: Morgan C. W. & Peterson

R. A. (editors) *Hell under fire: Modern Scholarship Reinvents Eternal Punishment,* Grand Rapids, Michigan: Zondervan.

Park, A. (1991) *You have called us chosen,* Mercy/Vineyard Publishing.

Pawson, D. (1990) *Leadership is Male,* Thomas Nelson Inc.

Pawson, D. (1996a), *The Road to Hell: Everlasting Torment or Annihilation,* Hodder & Stoughton Religious.

Pawson, D. (1996b) *Once Saved Always Saved?* Hodder & Stoughton Religious.

Riddle, J. (2011) *Furious,* Mercy/Vineyard Publishing. Available at: <http://jeremyriddle.net/wp-content/uploads/2011/10/Furious-Chords.pdf> [Accessed 2 May 2014].

Strobel, L. (2004) *The case for a Creator,* Grand Rapids, Michigan: Zondervan.

Strong's Greek Concordance. Available at: <http://biblehub.com/greek/strongs>. [Accessed 25 July 2014]

Warren, E. (2003) "Awake Me" from the album *Liquid Prayers,* Milton Keynes: Authentic Music.

Wesley C. *Love Divine All Loves Excelling.*

White, M. (1999) *Who was the Bloodiest Tyrant of the 20th Century.* Available at <http://necrometrics.com/tyrants.htm>. [Accessed 25 February 2011]

Willard, D. (1998) *The Divine Conspiracy,* London: Fount Paperbacks.

Wright, N.T. (2000) *The challenge of Jesus,* London: SPCK.

Wright, N.T. (2002) *John for Everyone, part 2,* London: SPCK.

Wright, N.T. (2007) *Surprised by Hope,* London: SPCK.

Index of Scriptures Cited

The figure in bold type indicates the chapter and sub-section in which the reference can be found.

Exodus

Exod. 3.1-3 – **5.0**
Exod. 3.1-4 – **4.3**
Exod. 13.21 – **4.3**
Exod. 19 – **5.0**
Exod. 19.18 – **4.3**
Exod. 24.17 – **4.3**
Exod. 34.5-6 – **10.3**
Exod. 34.5-7 – **10.5**
Exod. 34.6-7 – **8.0, 10.2**

Leviticus

Lev. 6.1-7 – **4.2**
Lev. 6.12-13 – **4.1**
Lev. 11 – **4.2**
Lev. 17.11 – **4.2**

Deuteronomy

Deut. 4.1, 15-37 – **15.2**
Deut. 4.23-24 – **5.0**
Deut. 4.24 – **2.4**
Deut. 32.21 – **7.2**

1 Kings

1 Kings 18.36-39 – **4.3**
1 Kings 19.11-12 – **4.3**
1 Kings 19.12 – **5.0**

Psalms

Ps. 14.2 – **3.0**

Ps. 16.10 – **2.1**
Ps. 18.8 – **4.3**
Ps. 19.1-2 – **12.3**
Ps. 19.4 – **7.2**
Ps. 43.3 – **7.2**
Ps. 63.1 – **14.3**
Ps. 66.10 – **6.0**
Ps. 80.14 – **3.0**
Ps. 102.19 – **3.0**
Ps. 102.25-27 – **5.0**
Ps. 103.1-5 – **7.1**
Ps. 136 – **10.5**
Ps. 141.1-2 – **4.2**

Proverbs
Prov. 7.27 – **2.1**

Isaiah
Isa. 11.1, 9 – **14.3**
Isa. 11.9 – **3.2**
Isa. 30.27, 30 – **4.3**
Isa. 33.14 – **4.3**
Isa. 41.17-20 – **14.3**
Isa. 48.10-11 – **6.0**
Isa. 65.1-2 – **7.2**
Isa. 65.17 – **3.2**
Isa. 66.22-24 – **2.3**

Jeremiah
Jer. 9.6 – **2.3**

Matt. 16.18 – **2.2**
Matt 18.8 – **3.2**
Matt. 18.9 – **2.2, 2.3**
Matt. 23.15, 33 – **2.2, 2.3**
Matt. 24.35 – **5.0**
Matt. 25.31-46 – **12.3, 13.0, 13.1, 13.2, 13.4, 15.1**
Matt. 25.34 – **14.0**
Matt 25.41 – **3.2**
Matt. 25.46 – **3.2, 5.0, 10.1, 13.3, 14.0**
Matt. 26.1 – **13.0**

Mark
Mark 5.12 – **9.3**
Mark 9.43-48 – **4.0**
Mark 9.43, 45, 47 – **2.2, 2.3**
Mark 9.48 – **2.3, 5.0**

Luke
Luke 4.16-21 – **3.1**
Luke 10.15 – **2.2**
Luke 12.5 – **2.2, 2.3**
Luke 14-16 – **4.4**
Luke 14.18-20 – **4.4**
Luke 15.11-32 – **10.2**
Luke 16.19-31 – **4.4**
Luke 16.23 – **2.2**
Luke 18.13 – **7.2**
Luke 23.34 – **10.4**

John

John 1.5 – **10.3**
John 3.16 – **10.2**
John 5.1-18 – **12.0**
John 5.19-29 – **12.1, 12.2, 12.3, 15.1**
John 5.25, 28 – **9.3**
John 5.29 – **9.3**
John 11.23-25 – **12.3**
John 14.5-6 – **7.2**
John 14.8-9 – **10.4**
John 17.3 – **14.4**
John 20.27 – **9.0**
John 21.4-14 – **9.0**

Acts

Acts 1.8 – **7.2**
Acts 2.27, 31 – **2.2**
Acts 4.12 – **7.2**
Acts 10 – **4.2**
Acts 15.19-29 – **4.2**
Acts 24.15 – **9.3**

Romans

Rom. 3.28 – **13.1**
Rom. 6.23 – **8.2**
Rom. 8.18-21 – **3.2**
Rom. 8.22 – **14.0**
Rom. 10.14-18 – **7.2**
Rom. 12.1 – **4.2**

1 Corinthians
1 Cor. 3.12-15 – **6.0**
1 Cor. 13.4-7 – **10.2**
1 Cor. 13.12 – **14.4**
1 Cor. 13.13 – **2.4**
1 Cor. 15 – **7.1, 9.0**
1 Cor. 15.20 – **9.0**
1 Cor. 15.23, 36-37 – **9.0**
1 Cor. 15.37 – **14.0**
1 Cor. 15.42-54 – **9.1**
1 Cor. 15.50 – **9.3**
1 Cor. 15.57 – **9.2**

2 Corinthians
2 Cor. 4.18 – **3.2**
2 Cor. 5.1 – **3.2**
2 Cor. 5.2-3 – **9.2**

Galatians
Gal. 5.22-23 – **10.4**

Ephesians
Eph. 2.8 – **7.2**
Eph. 2.8-9 – **13.1**
Eph. 2.19 – **4.2**

2 Thessalonians
2 Thes. 1.9 – **3.2**

1 Timothy
1 Tim. 6.16 – **3.2**

2 Timothy
2 Tim. 3.16-17 - **introduction**

Hebrews
Heb. 6.2 – **3.2**
Heb. 10.1 – **4.1**
Heb. 12.1, 18-29 – **15.2**
Heb. 12.22 – **7.2**
Heb. 12.22-24 – **7.2**
Heb. 12.22-29 – **4.4, 5.0**
Heb. 12.28-29 – **2.4**
Heb. 12.29 – **2.4, 10.3**

James
Jas. 3.6 – **2.2, 2.3**

1 Peter
1 Pet. 5.10 – **3.2**

2 Peter
2 Pet. 2.4 – **2.2**
2 Pet. 3.12-13 – **6.0**

1 John
1 John 1.5 – **10.3**
1 John 4.7-12, 16 – **10.5**
1 John 4.8, 16 – **10.3, 10.5**
1 John 4.9-10 – **10.3**

Jude
Jude 1.7 – **3.2**

Revelation

Lightning Source UK Ltd.
Milton Keynes UK
UKOW05f2236181214

243344UK00001B/12/P